In Search of
Bible
Trivia

Bob Phillips

HARVEST HOUSE PUBLISHERS
Eugene, Oregon 97402

All Scripture quotations are taken from the King James Version of the Bible.

Cover by Terry Dugan Design, Minneapolis, Minnesota

IN SEARCH OF BIBLE TRIVIA
(Formerly *In Pursuit of Bible Trivia*)
Copyright © 1985 by Harvest House Publishers
Eugene, Oregon 97402

Library of Congress Catalog Card Number 84-082351
ISBN 0-7369-0696-7

Printed in the United States of America.

01 02 03 04 05 / BC-BG / 10 9 8 7 6

*To my wife Pam
and my daughters, Lisa and Christy,
and to all who enjoy the little-known facts
of the Bible.*

Contents

Facts & Fun

For a number of years I have collected unusual Bible facts, Bible puns, and riddles to share with friends and to add a little sparkle to sermons. The renewed interest in various kinds of trivia prompted me to compile this fun collection of well-known and little-known Bible facts. Also included is a section on humorous Bible puns and riddles.

In Search of Bible Trivia can be utilized in a number of different ways:

◆ You can read it just for your own personal amusement and review of your Bible knowledge. It is designed in such a way that you can write down your answers to the questions.

◆ You can use the unusual facts to add interest and humor to your public speaking.

◆ You can use the book as a tool to help pass the time while traveling as a family. Many of the facts will spark discussion about Bible events and stories.

◆ You can utilize the little-known facts as an ice-breaker at various get-togethers.

◆ You can take various questions in the book and use them as part of a Biblical Pursuit game with a small group of friends.

◆ You can share the questions on a large group or team basis also. Questions along with the answers are repeated in the back of the book. This was done in the event you would like to ask questions of a group and have an immediate answer ready. You will find a large group game like this to be much fun for everyone.

As you read *In Search of Bible Trivia*, I hope you will have as much fun answering the questions as I did in compiling them.

—*Bob Phillips*
Hume, California

In Search of
Bible
Trivia

Easy Trivia Questions

1. How many men did Nebuchadnezzar see walking in the fiery furnace?

   _____

2. What did Noah see in the sky?

   _____

3. "For whatsoever a man soweth,_____
   _____"

4. "But_____found grace in the eyes of the Lord."

5. "Delilah said to _____ , Tell me, I pray thee, wherein thy great strength lieth."

6. "Pride goeth before destruction, and a haughty spirit before _____."

7. "Follow me and I will make you _____
   _____."

8. "Come unto me, all ye that labor and are _____
   _____"

9. What were the names of the three disciples who were on the Mount of Transfiguration with Jesus?

   _____

10. What was the name of the village that was known as the "City of David"?

_____

11. Who was Andrew's brother?

_____

12. "A soft answer turneth away _____."

13. The disciples were told to be wise as _____and harmless as_____.

14. In what city did Joseph, Mary, and Jesus live?

_____

15. What country did Joseph, Mary, and Jesus flee to?

_____

16. Where did the Wise Men come from?

_____

17. In the parable of the ten virgins, how many were wise and how many were foolish?

_____

18. Where did Jesus perform His first miracle?

_____

19. John the Baptist had an interesting diet of what?

_____

20. In what book of the Bible do you find these words? "I am the living bread which came down from heaven; if any man eat of this bread, he shall live for ever."

_____

21. Peter said to Jesus, "Thou shalt never wash ____."

a. My hands   b. My feet   c. My hair
d. My clothes   e. My cup

22. Who prayed three times a day at an open window?

_____

23. Who had an occupation as a tentmaker?

_____

24. Jesus was arrested in _____.

25. Who in the Bible could be called "The Lion Tamer"?

_____

26. John the Baptist was how much older than Jesus?

_____

27. Who in the Bible could carry the title "The Strong Man"?

_____

28. "If God be for us, _____
_____?"

29. In what book of the Bible do you find the words, "There is no new thing under the sun"?

_____

30. According to the book of Proverbs, the beginning of knowledge is _____.

31. Who was the man who said, "Every kind of beasts, and of birds hath been tamed by mankind"?

_____

32. In what book of the Bible do you find the story of the burning bush?

_____

33. To whom did Jesus say, "Get thee behind me, Satan"?

_____

34. Who prayed inside of a fish?

_____

35. What is the longest psalm in the Bible?

_____

36. The wise man built his house on _____ and the foolish man built his house on _____.

37. What was the name of the special food that God provided for the children of Israel during the forty years in the wilderness?

_____

38. "I am _____ and _____, the beginning and the ending."

39. In what book of the Bible do you find the following words? "And there are also many other things which Jesus did, the which, if they should be written every one, I suppose that even the world itself could not contain the books that should be written."

_____

40. Who in the Bible could carry the title "The Wise King"?

_____

41. Bartimaeus was:

a. Lame b. Deaf c. Blind d. Leprous

42. Who owned a coat that had many colors?

_____

43. "I am the true _____ , and my Father is the husbandman."

44. What Bible character was turned into a pillar of salt?

_____

45. What Bible character ate food that was given to the pigs?

_____

46. What type of animal did Aaron fashion out of gold?

_____

47. In what book of the Bible do you find the following words? "In my Father's house are many mansions."

_____

48. Who wrote with His finger on the ground?

_____

49. Name the three gifts that the Wise Men from the East brought to baby Jesus.

_____

50. "For what shall it profit a man, if he shall gain____

_____?"

51. How many books are in the New Testament?

    a. 23   b. 25   c. 27   d. 29

52. "Pray without _____."

53. Where in the Bible do you find the following words? "Behold, I stand at the door, and knock."

_____

54. Who said, "Silver or gold have I none, but such as I have give I thee"?

_____

55. What is the first lie to be recorded in the Bible?

_____

56. "I can do all things through _____."

57. How many books are in the Old Testament?

    a. 33   b. 35   c. 37   d. 39

58. The book of Hebrews tells us to entertain strangers because they might be _____.

59. "Let the word of Christ dwell in you _____."

60. "Whatsoever ye do in word or deed, do all _____
_____."

61. "The _____ of a good man are ordered by the Lord."

62. "I am the good _____."

63. "Be not overcome of evil, but_____
_____."

64. "I am the _____ of the _____."

65. "I am the _____, the _____, and the_____."

66. "I am the _____; by me if any man enter in, he shall be saved."

67. "If thy right eye offend thee, _____."

68. Who in the Bible was called, "A man after mine own heart"?

_____

69. Who said, "Every son that is born ye shall cast into the river, and every daughter ye shall save alive"?

_____

70. To whom was the following said? "Loose thy shoe from off thy foot; for the place whereon thou standest is holy."

_____

71. "_____, and it shall be given you; _____, and yet shall find; _____, and it will be opened unto you."

72. Who said, "When I was a child, I spake as a child, I understood as a child, I thought as a child"?

_____

73. Who said, "How can a man be born when he is old"?

_____

74. "For the wages of sin is death; _____

_____."

75. Who said, "By their fruits ye shall know them"?

_____

76. Who said, "Almost thou persuadest me to be a Christian"?

_____

77. In what book in the Bible do you find the following? "So Joseph died, being a hundred and ten years old."

_____

78. Who said, "Who touched my clothes?"

_____

79. Of whom was the following spoken? "He was a murderer from the beginning, and abode not in the truth, because there is no truth in him."

_____

80. What was the name of Abraham's wife?

_____

81. In what book of the Bible do you find the laws concerning the eating of clean things?

_____

82. In what book of the Bible do you find the phrase, "God is love"?

_____

83. "Thy word is a lamp unto my feet, and _____
_____."

84. "For many are called, _____
_____."

85. What is the shortest verse in the New Testament?

_____

86. "O death, where is thy sting?_____
_____?"

87. How did Judas indicate to the crowd who Jesus was?

_____

88. Who in the Bible could be called "Mr. Patience"?

_____

89. To whom were the following words spoken? "Because thou has done this, thou are cursed."

_____

90. David's occupation before he became a king was

_____.

91. "And ye shall know the truth, and the truth shall
_____."

92. What is greater than faith and hope?

_____

93. What happens when the blind lead the blind?

_____

94. To whom was the following comment made? "For God so loved the world, that he gave his only begotten Son, that whosoever believeth in him should not perish, but have everlasting life."

_____

95. "For where two or three are gathered together in my name, _____."

96. In what book of the Bible do you find the following words? "Let every thing that hath breath praise the Lord."

_____

97. Cain did what for a living?

_____

98. Peter did what for a living?

_____

99. Which apostle was called Doubting _____?

100. Abel did what for a living?

_____

101. Joseph, the husband of Mary, did what for a living?

_____

102. In what book of the Bible do you find the words, "Blessed is the man that walketh not in the counsel of the ungodly"?

_____

103. "Speak; for thy servant _____."

104. In what book of the Bible do you find the words, "In the beginning was the Word and the Word was with God, and the Word was God"?

_____

105. "The Lord is my strength and _____."

106. Who said that even all the hairs on our head are numbered by God?

_____

107. Paul told Timothy to take something for his stomach's sake. What was it?

_____

108. "Greater love hath no man than this, _____
_____."

109. When did Jesus make more than a hundred gallons of very good wine?

_____

110. Who made clothes out of leaves that were sewed together?

_____

111. Who was the wife of Boaz?

_____

112. Who in the Bible could be called "The Giant Killer"?

_____

113. Who was the oldest brother—Cain or Abel?

_____

114. Who gave Jesus some food to help feed the 5000?

_____

115. Who said, "My soul doth magnify the Lord . . . he hath regarded the low estate of his handmaiden . . . all generations shall call me blessed"?

_____

116. Who said that, "I have fought a good fight, I have finished my course, I have kept the faith"?

_____

117. What was the name of the man who gave each man in his army of 300 a trumpet and an empty pitcher?

_____

118. Who took golden earrings and made them into a calf?

_____

119. Jesus said, "Peace, be still." Whom was He addressing?

120. "Saul hath slain his thousands, and David his ____

    _____."

121. What was Paul's other name?

122. Jesus mixed something with clay and put it on the eyes of the blind man to make him see. What did Jesus mix with the clay?

123. When the Roman soldiers pierced Jesus in the side with a spear, what came out?

124. "For what is a man profited, if he shall gain the whole world, and lose his own _____?"

125. Did Judas Iscariot keep the betrayal money or did he give it back?

126. The Spirit of God descended on Jesus in the form of a_____.

127. "For the law was given by Moses, but grace and _____ came by Jesus Christ."

128. What did Ananias sell in order to get money to give to the apostles?

129. Who said, "No prophet is accepted in his own country"?

130. Water that Jesus turned into wine was in how many pots?

131. Who was Jesus talking about when He said, "I have not found so great a faith, no, not in Israel"?

_____

132. "Go ye therefore, and teach all nations, baptizing them_____."

133. "Judge not, _____."

134. Who brought back to life the son of the widow in whose house he was staying?

_____

Fairly Easy Trivia Questions

1. What was the name of the prophet who was very hairy and wore a leather belt?

   _____

2. What is the name of the man who King David arranged to have killed because he wanted his wife?

   _____

3. The earth, seas, grass, herb yielding seed, and the tree yielding fruit were created on which day of creation?

   a. 2nd   b. 3rd   c. 4th   d. 5th

4. What was the name of the man who inherited Elijah's mantle?

   _____

5. What was the name of the man who owned a seamless coat?

   _____

6. What was the name of a man who worked seven years to earn a wife?

   _____

7. What Bible prophet said, "Behold, a virgin shall conceive, and bear a son, and shall call his name Immanuel"?

8. How old was Joseph when he was given his coat of many colors?

9. What was the name of the high priest's servant who had his ear cut off by the apostle Peter?

10. What was the name of the Bible character who was blind and killed 3000 people while at a religious feast?

11. What was the name of the Jewish man who called himself greater than King Solomon?

12. After David knocked Goliath to the ground with a stone from his sling, he cut off Goliath's head with his own sword. True or false?

13. What nation of people got sick and tired of eating quail for dinner?

14. Which came first—the plague of lice or the plague of frogs?

15. What was the name of the Bible prophet who was fed by birds?

16. About whom was the following statement made?

"Among those that are born of women there is not a greater prophet than . . ."?

17. On what mountain did Noah's Ark come to rest?

18. What was the name of the queen who came from a far country to witness for herself the wisdom of King Solomon?

19. What was the name of the man who wore clothes made out of camel's hair?

20. At whose command were 300 pitchers broken?

21. How many days was Saul blind while in Damascus?

22. Who were the people who found frogs on their beds and in their ovens?

23. Who said, "Divide the living child in two, and give half to the one, and half to the other"?

24. What was the name of the Bible character who was a cupbearer to a king and also an engineer?

25. What was the name of the man who came to Jesus by night to talk with him?

26. How old was Methuselah when he died?

_____

27. Name the fruit of the Spirit.

_____

28. How many windows were in Noah's Ark?

_____

29. What was the name of the man who was released from prison by an angel?

_____

30. In what book of the Bible do you find the words, "Of making many books there is no end"?

_____

31. What were the names of the two disciples who were called, "The Sons of Thunder"?

_____

32. In order to see Jesus more clearly, Zacchaeus climbed what type of tree?

_____

33. What was the name of the man who escaped from Damascus in a basket?

_____

34. How many people were saved in Noah's Ark?

_____

35. What was the name of the man who issued the decree that all the world should be taxed?

_____

36. What was the name of the tree that Adam and Eve were told not to eat fruit from?

_____

37. What was the name of the man who foretold of the seven good years and the seven lean years in Egypt?

_____

38. What was the name of the first woman judge in Israel?

_____

39. What was the name of the couple who died because they lied to the Holy Spirit?

_____

40. Who was accused of eating in the cornfields on the Sabbath?

_____

41. The Israelites were bitten by _____ and were healed by looking at the same creature made out of brass.

42. Moses had a brother. What was his name?

_____

43. How many times did Samuel go to Eli the priest, thinking that Eli had called him?

_____

44. What was the name of the queen who was devoured by dogs?

_____

45. How old was Joseph when his brothers sold him into slavery?

_____

46. What is the name of the angel who told Mary that she would be the mother of Jesus?

_____

47. How many years did the children of Israel eat manna?

_____

48. How many years did God give Noah to build the Ark?

_____

49. How many stories or levels were in the Ark?

_____

50. What was the name of the father who was struck dumb, because of unbelief, until his son was born?

_____

51. What was the name of the man who had to work many years and got two wives as a result?

_____

52. What was in the Ark in the Tabernacle?

_____

53. The Bible talks of a very tiny seed that becomes a very large tree. What is the name of the seed?

_____

54. How many Marys are mentioned in the Bible?

_____

55. What was the name of the woman who was called "The Seller of Purple"?

_____

56. What is the last line of the Twenty-third Psalm?

_____

57. Jesus said that He would rebuild the temple in how many days?

_____

58. The manger is to Jesus as the basket in the bulrushes is to_____.

59. Who said, "Repent ye: for the kingdom of heaven is at hand"?

_____

60. On what mountain did Moses receive the law?

_____

61. Who replaced Moses as the leader of the children of Israel?

_____

62. To whom was the following statement made? "Take nothing for your journey, neither staves, nor scrip, neither bread, neither money; neither have two coats apiece."

_____

63. Timothy's mother was a Jewess and his father was

_____.

64. What color was Esau's complexion?　　a. Pale
    b. Light brown　　c. Red　　d. Black　　e. White

65. What color was the robe that Jesus wore when the soldiers taunted Him?

_____

66. Genesis is to Malachi as Matthew is to_____.

67. Matthew, Mark, and John called it Golgotha or the place of the skull. What did Luke call it?

_____

68. In what book of the Bible do you find the words, "Make haste, my beloved, and be thou like to a roe or to a young hart upon the mountains of spices"?

_____

69. In what book of the Bible do you find the words, "Be strong and of a good courage"?   a. Job
b. Philippians   c. Joshua   d. Ephesians

70. Who said, "I am innocent of the blood of this just person"?

_____

71. How many hours was Jesus on the cross?

_____

72. What was the relationship of Zebedee to James and John?

_____

73. In what book of the Bible do you find the words, "Blessed are the meek: for they shall inherit the earth"?

_____

74. In what book of the Bible do you find the Ten Commandments?

_____

75. Who said, "He was oppressed, and he was afflicted, yet he opened not his mouth"?   a. Isaiah
b. Jeremiah   c. Ezekiel   d. Hosea

76. Who was born first—Jacob or Esau?

_____

77. The spies who spied out the land of Canaan said that it flowed with _____ and _____.

78. Who was stoned to death for preaching that Jesus was the Savior?

_____

79. "It is easier for a _____ to go through the eye of a _____, than for a _____ to enter into the kingdom of God."

80. In the parable of the ten virgins, five of them were wise and five were foolish. Why were the foolish ones foolish?

81. Who were the disciples who argued about sitting on the right- and left-hand sides of Jesus?

82. Who witnessed the conversation between Moses, Elijah, and Jesus?

83. On what day of creation were the sun, the moon, and the stars created?

84. Paul and Barnabas had an argument over a certain man traveling with them on their missionary journey. What was that man's name?

85. What were the names of the two spies who spied out Canaan Land and gave a favorable report?

86. What Bible character was renamed Israel?

87. What preacher was mad because his preaching caused a whole city to repent?

88. On what day of creation were the sea creatures and fowl created?

89. Who saw Satan fall from heaven?

90. Who had a wrestling match with God and won?

91. Which came first, "Thou shalt not kill" or "Thou shalt not steal"?

92. What was the name of the apostle who was ship-wrecked three different times?

93. On which day of creation were the land animals and man created?

94. What Bible character had 300 concubines?

95. What was the name of a physician in the Bible who was also an author?

96. Who sold their younger brother into slavery?

97. Lot escaped from the city of Sodom with whom?

98. What was the name of the man who ordered the execution of 450 priests?

99. Which book in the Bible was written to an "Elect Lady"?

100. Jesus said that it was proper to pay tribute (money) to what man?

101. Simon Peter cut off the ear of the high priest's servant. Which ear did he cut off?

_____

102. What Bible character said, "A little leaven leaveneth the whole lump"?

_____

103. How many years did Jacob work for his Uncle Laban in payment for his daughters?

_____

104. Who was healed—the son or the daughter of Jairus?

_____

105. "Blessed are the pure in heart: _____."

106. What book in the Bible has a warning against anyone adding to it or taking away from it?

_____

107. What was the name of the man who lifted up the infant Jesus at the temple and praised God?

_____

108. In what book of the Bible do you find the following: "For the Lord himself shall descend from heaven with a shout, with the voice of the archangel"?

_____

109. What sign was given to the shepherds at the time of Christ's birth?

_____

110. How many loaves and how many fishes did Jesus use to feed the 5000?

_____

111. For what reason did the rich young ruler come to Christ?

_____

112. What does the name Emmanuel mean?

_____

113. What was the name of the king who sought to take the life of the baby Jesus?

_____

114. What was the name of the criminal who was released in place of Jesus?

_____

115. What was the name of the mother of Abraham's first son?

_____

116. What Bible character had a dream that his parents and brothers would bow down before him?

_____

117. The city walls of _____ fell down when the trumpets were blown.

118. Name the two bodies of water that the children of Israel crossed on dry ground.

_____

119. Where in the Bible do you find the longest recorded prayer of Jesus?

_____

120. What was Matthew's other name?

_____

121. What is the first beatitude?

_____

122. Is Bethlehem located in Galilee or in Judea?

123. Jesus said that there were two masters you could not serve at the same time. What were they?

124. What was Sarah's other name?

125. Who said, "Am I my brother's keeper?"

126. Who said, "The Lord gave, and the Lord hath taken away; blessed be the name of the Lord"?

127. Who owned a coat that was dipped in blood?

128. Who was bitten by a snake and shook it off into a fire and felt no harm?

129. Peter was told by Jesus to forgive his brother how many times?

Fairly Difficult Trivia Questions

1. Name the man who kept some of the spoils after the battle of Jericho and brought punishment to Israel.

   _____

2. How many of Jesus' brothers wrote books of the Bible?

   _____

3. What was the name of Hosea's wife?

   _____

4. What woman in the Bible tried to seduce a handsome slave?

   _____

5. What was the name of the king who made a speech and as a result was eaten by worms?

   _____

6. Miriam and Aaron were upset with Moses because he married a woman who was an _____.

7. How many of the clean animals did Noah take into the Ark?

   _____

8. What was the name of a Bible character who told a riddle about a lion?

9. There was a very rich man who was a disciple of Jesus. What was his name?

10. What was the name of the queen who was thrown out of a window?

11. Solomon said that something "biteth like a serpent, stingeth like an adder." What was it?

12. What was the name of the city where King Ahasuerus lived?

13. David is to a sling as Samson is to _____.

14. How many times did Noah send the dove from the Ark?

15. Who had shoes that lasted for forty years and did not wear out?

16. What is the name of the father who had two daughters married to the same man?

17. How many years were the Israelites in bondage as slaves?

18. King Solomon had how many wives?

19. Name the two men who entertained angels unaware.

20. What was the name of the prophet who was swept away by a whirlwind?

21. The Sabeans took his oxen and his donkeys, the lightning killed his sheep, the Chaldeans stole his camels, and his servants were killed. To whom did all these things happen?

22. Who dreamed about a ladder which reached up to heaven?

23. To whom were the following words addressed? "Get thee out of thy country, and from thy kindred, and from thy father's house, unto a land that I will shew thee."

24. What Bible character was called "The Gloomy Prophet"?

25. The man called Gehazi was a: a. Prophet b. Servant c. King d. Lawyer e. Wicked priest

26. What is the name of the first of the twelve disciples to be murdered?

27. David the shepherd was how old when he became King of Israel?

28. Who owned dishes that were pure gold?

   _____

29. Someone came to Pilate and begged for the body of the crucified Jesus. Who was he?

   _____

30. In what book of the Bible do you find the following words? "For God shall bring every work into judgment, with every secret thing, whether it be good, or whether it be evil."

   _____

31. What was Lot's relationship with Abraham?

   _____

32. What is the name of the town that is called "City of Palm Trees"?

   _____

33. Shem is to Noah as David is to _____.

34. What was Jacob's relationship to Laban?

   _____

35. What is the name of the first New Testament martyr?

   _____

36. Name the pool that had five porches.

   _____

37. Which came first—the Tower of Babel or the Flood?

   _____

38. Lazarus is to Jesus as Eutychus is to _____.

39. There was a silversmith in Ephesus by the name of

   _____

40. What is the name of the Bible character that preached in a valley full of dead men's bones?

   _____

41. How old was Joseph when Pharaoh made him a ruler?

   _____

42. Apollos was a: a. King   b. God
   c. Learned Jew   d. Maker of tents

43. What was the name of the man who helped an African to understand the Scriptures?

   _____

44. What Bible character used salt to purify drinking water?

   _____

45. How old was Moses when he died?

   _____

46. Something very special happened to a certain man when he was 600 years old. Who was he and what happened?

   _____

47. How many times did the boy who Elisha raised from the dead sneeze?

   _____

48. The Ark that Noah built was thirty cubits high, fifty cubits wide, and _____ cubits long.

49. Who said, "This day is this scripture fulfilled in your ears"?

   _____

50. What Bible character ate a poor widow's last meal?

   _____

51. In what book of the Bible does it describe hail-stones weighing a talent each (about 80 pounds)?

52. How many years did it take to build the temple in Jesus' time?

53. Who was the man who ordered a cup to be put into a sack of corn?

54. There are two orders of angels. Can you name them?

55. Some angels came to speak with Lot. How many angels were there?

56. How many psalms are there in the Old Testament?

57. What is the name of the Bible character whose handkerchiefs were used to heal people?

58. Joab was a: a. Scribe   b. Priest
    c. King   d. Soldier   e. Servant

59. What is the name of the man who was called "The Supplanter"?

60. What relationship was Mordecai to Esther?

61. What is the name of the boy who was sent out into the desert with his mother?

62. What is the name of the man who offered thirty changes of garments for solving a riddle?

63. What was the name of a leper who was also the captain of the host of the King of Syria?

64. Who asked for the head of John the Baptist and got it?

65. What are the three most famous heads of hair mentioned in the Bible?

66. What was the name of the Egyptian who bought Joseph from the Midianites?

67. One of Joseph's brothers said, "Let us not kill him." Who was that brother?

68. Who could be called the great hunter of the Bible? (He also loved red meat.)

69. The Gibeonites would have been killed by Joshua if it had not been for their old clothes, old shoes, and what kind of bread?

70. When Joseph's brothers first came to Egypt, he put them into jail for: a. 1 day   b. 2 days   c. 3 days   d. 4 days   e. 5 days   f. 6 days

71. How many Herods are there in the Bible?

72. What type of wood did Noah use when he built the Ark?

_____

73. How many elders did Moses appoint to help him share the load of dealing with the children of Israel?

_____

74. Who wrote the book of Lamentations?

_____

75. What three young men had a father who was 500 years old?

_____

76. There was a certain group of men who could not wear garments that would cause them to sweat. Who were these men?

_____

77. Abraham asked God to spare the city of Sodom if a certain number of righteous people lived there. What was the final figure that God said He would spare the city for?

_____

78. In whose tomb was Jesus buried?

_____

79. What was the name of the woman who cast her young son in the bushes to die?

_____

80. What was the name of the mother who hid her son in the bulrushes?

_____

81. Jesus cursed three cities. What were their names?

_____

82. What was the name of the country in which Jesus healed two demon-possessed individuals?

_____

83. How many loaves of bread did Jesus use in feeding the 4000?

_____

84. Abraham left what country?

_____

85. When Philip met the Ethiopian eunuch, he was reading from what book in the Old Testament?

_____

86. Paul preached on Mars' Hill. In what city is Mars' Hill located?

_____

87. Into how many parts did the soldiers divide Jesus' garments?

_____

88. What was the name of Jacob's firstborn child?

_____

89. When Jacob followed Esau out of his mother's womb, he was holding onto what?

_____

90. What happened to Jacob when he wrestled with God?

_____

91. How many times did the children of Israel march around the city of Jericho?   a. 2   b. 7   c. 13   d. 21   e. 49

92. What was the name of the wilderness in which John the Baptist preached?

_____

93. What caused the large fish to vomit Jonah onto dry land?

94. Who cast down his rod before Pharaoh and the rod became a serpent?

95. Who said, "The dog is turned to his own vomit again"?

96. "At midnight _____ and _____ prayed, and sang praises unto God; and the prisoners heard them."

97. God opened the mouth of a donkey and the donkey spoke to _____.

98. What was the name of the centurion from Caesarea who was part of the Italian band?

99. What was the name of Aquila's wife?

100. What was the name of the man who carried the cross for Jesus?

101. To whom was the following spoken? "Go near, and join thyself to this chariot."

102. What was the name of Timothy's mother?

103. Paul the Apostle was born in what city?

104. What was the name of the prophet who foretold that Jesus would be born in Bethlehem?

_____

105. What relationship was Lois to Timothy?

_____

106. "As it is written, _____ have I loved, but _____ have I hated."

107. What is the name of the Old Testament prophet who foretold the virgin birth?

_____

108. To whom was the following spoken? "Silver and gold have I none; but such as I have give I thee: In the name of Jesus Christ of Nazareth rise up and walk."

_____

109. What is the name of the woman who hid two Israelite spies on the roof of her house?

_____

110. What Bible character saw a city coming down out of heaven?

_____

Hard Trivia Questions

1. Who was hung on a gallows fifty cubits (about seventy-five feet) high?

   _____

2. What were the names of the first and last judges of Israel?

   _____

3. Who was the individual who watched over baby Moses while he floated in the bulrushes?

   _____

4. What was the name of the mother who made a little coat for her son every year?

   _____

5. What Bible prophet spoke of the killing of the children?

   _____

6. What type of bird did Noah first send forth from the Ark?

   _____

7. The name of David's first wife was _____.

8. The title written above Jesus' cross said, "JESUS

OF NAZARETH THE KING OF THE JEWS."
Name the three languages that the title was written
in.

_____

9. Because of Achan's sin he was stoned in the valley
   of _____.

10. What was the name of the sorcerer who was struck
    blind by Paul the apostle?

    _____

11. After Paul's shipwreck he swam to the island of____

    _____.

12. What was the name of the wife of both Nabal and
    King David?

    _____

13. Which of Joseph's brothers was left behind as a
    hostage when the other nine returned to bring
    Benjamin to Egypt?

    _____

14. In order to win the battle with Amalek, Aaron and
    Hur helped Moses by _____.

15. Zipporah had a very famous husband. What was
    his name?

    _____

16. What was the name of the wife of Lapidoth and
    what is she famous for?

    _____

17. When David scrabbled on the doors of the gate,
    and let spittle fall down on his beard, and pre-
    tended to be crazy, he was doing so because he was
    afraid of _____.

18. In what book of the Bible do you find: "As a jewel of gold in a swine's snout . . ."?

_____

19. What was Nebuchadnezzar's son's name?

_____

20. "The Lord had made all things for himself: yea, even the wicked for _____."

21. Hannah was the mother of Samuel. What was the name of Hannah's husband?

_____

22. Whom did God tell to go and marry a prostitute?

_____

23. What is the name of the Bible character who saw a roll flying in the sky?

_____

24. Two men in the Bible had the same name. One was a very poor man and the other was a friend of Jesus. What was their common name?

_____

25. When Peter was released from prison, he knocked at the door of the gate and a certain person came to answer his knock. Who was that individual?

_____

26. People will be thrown into the lake of fire because

_____.

27. When Paul was shipwrecked on the island of Melita, he stayed with the chief man on the island. Who was this man?

_____

28. What is the name of the man who slept in the land of Nod?

_____

29. "And they gave forth their lots; and the lot fell upon _____; and he was numbered with the eleven apostles."

30. What was the name of the vagabond Jewish exorcists who tried to cast the evil spirit out of a man? "And the man in whom the evil spirit was leaped on them, and overcame them, and prevailed against them, so that they fled out of that house naked and wounded."

_____

31. "And Cush begat _____. He was a mighty hunter before the Lord."

32. What was the name of the queen that was replaced by Esther?

_____

33. What Bible character was called "The Tishbite"?

_____

34. Who in the Bible asked God to put his tears in a bottle?

_____

35. What was the name of the archangel who debated with the devil?

_____

36. What does the word Ichabod mean?

_____

37. The apostle Peter was known by three other names. What were they?

_____

38. What was the name of the runaway slave who went back to his master?

_____

39. Who said, "Am I a dog, that thou comest to me with staves"?

_____

40. What is the name of the partially blind man who was ninety-eight years old and was very fat who fell off his seat and broke his neck?

_____

41. What is the shortest verse in the Bible?

_____

42. What Bible character accidentally hanged himself in a tree?

_____

43. How many children did Jacob have? a. 9
    b. 11   c. 13   d. 15   e. 17

44. How many days was Noah on the Ark before it started to rain?

_____

45. What type of bird fed the prophet Elijah?

_____

46. What is the longest chapter in the Bible?

_____

47. In what book of the Bible do you find the following words: "Can the Ethiopian change his skin, or the leopard his spots"?

_____

48. When a certain king put on a feast, God's hand-writing appeared on the wall and startled everyone present. What is the name of this king?

_____

49. What is the name of the woman who slept at the feet of her future husband?

_____

50. What type of food did the brothers of Joseph eat after they threw him into the pit?

_____

51. A scarlet cord in a window saved someone and their family. Who was this person?

_____

52. In a contest for good-looking men, four men won because they were vegetarians and God blessed them. Who were these men?

_____

53. Elisha cursed forty-two children because they made fun of him and mocked him. What did they say?

_____

54. As a result of the curse of Elisha, what happened to the forty-two children?

_____

55. When God expelled Adam and Eve from the Garden of Eden, he placed Cherubim at the _____ of the Garden of Eden.

56. What Bible character drove his chariot furiously?

_____

57. What is the name of the left-handed Benjamite who killed King Eglon?

_____

58. King Eglon was killed with a dagger that was _____ inches long, and the dagger could not be pulled out because _____.

59. What two books in the Bible were written to Theophilus?

_____

60. What Bible character had his lips touched with a live coal?

_____

61. Who was the person who dreamed about a tree which reached to heaven?

_____

62. What woman in the Bible had five husbands?

_____

63. When the Wise Men came to seek the baby Jesus, where did they find him?

_____

64. Who caused bricklayers to go on strike?

_____

65. What Bible character changed dust into lice?

_____

66. Who was the man to first organize an orchestra in the Bible?

_____

67. Of all the books in the Bible, which one does not contain the name of God?

_____

68. A lost ax head was made to float by _____

_____.

69. What person in the Bible walked for forty days without eating?

_____

70. Why did Absalom kill his brother Amnon?

_____

71. Who paid for the nursing of Moses?

_____

72. Who committed suicide with his own sword?

_____

73. Who committed suicide by hanging himself?

_____

74. What king pouted in his bed because he could not buy someone's vineyard?

_____

75. King Solomon had another name. What was it?

_____

76. Who was the man to build the first city and what was its name?

_____

77. What woman in the Bible made a pair of kid gloves for her son?

_____

78. A certain queen's blood was sprinkled on horses. Who was this queen?

_____

79. Who was the first musician in the Bible? What instruments did he play?

_____

80. What Bible person cut his hair only once a year?

_____

81. Name the gentile king that made Esther his queen.

82. Who said the following and to whom was he speaking? "Because thou hast mocked me: I would there were a sword in mine hand, for now would I kill thee."

83. The mother-in-law of Ruth was Naomi. What was the name of her father-in-law?

84. Which man committed adultry with his daughter-in-law after she disguised herself as a harlot? What was her name?

85. How many times did Balaam hit his donkey before the donkey spoke to him?

86. How many years were added to Hezekiah's life?

87. Joash was told to shoot an arrow from the window. What was the arrow called?

88. God gave Hezekiah a sign that he would live longer. What was that sign?

89. Name the king who had the longest reign in the Bible.

90. Which of the prophets was thrown into a dungeon?

91. When a certain king tried to take the place of the priest at the altar, he was struck with leprosy. Who was this king?

92. How was Naaman healed of his leprosy?

93. While _____ was hanging in a tree, he was killed by three darts from Joab.

94. Nicodemus put how many pounds of myrrh and aloes on the body of Jesus?

95. What was the name of the person who became king while he was a little child?

96. Job's friends sat in silence with Job and mourned with him for how many days?

97. Where was Judas Iscariot buried?

98. Jesus told Nathanael that he had seen him before. Where did Jesus see Nathanael?

99. In the book of Proverbs, God says He hates how many things?

100. The Bible suggests that the average life span is how many years?

101. How many barrels of water did Elijah ask the men to pour over the sacrifice on the altar?

102. Because of offering "strange fire" on the altar of God, how many men died?

103. David disobeyed God and numbered the people. As a result, how many punishment choices did God give David?

    a. 2   b. 3   c. 4   d. 5

104. What leader chose his followers by watching how they drank water?

105. How many stones were placed in the Jordan River after the children of Israel had crossed over on dry land?

106. As Joshua and the children of Israel marched around the walls of Jericho, the priests carried trumpets before the Ark of the Lord. How many priests carried trumpets?

107. When Elijah was on Mt. Carmel, how many times did he send his servant to look for a cloud?

108. The two spies that Rahab hid fled into the mountains and hid for how many days?

109. How many men from the tribe of Judah were sent out to capture Samson?

110. How old was Jehoash when he was crowned king?

111. This person was brought water from the well at Bethlehem but poured it out on the ground

because it was brought to him at great risk. Who was this person?

_____

112. What type of bird was sold for "two for a farthing"?

_____

113. Absalom was riding on a _____ when his hair caught in a tree.

114. What did Achan steal from Jericho?

_____

115. What Old Testament character wore a "coat of mail"?

_____

116. Name the twelve apostles.

_____

_____

117. What was the name of the witch that Saul visited?

_____

118. The word "coffin" is used only once in the entire Bible. Do you know who was buried in this coffin?

_____

119. The Bible warns men to beware of a woman's eyes. In what book of the Bible do you find this warning?

_____

120. While Joseph was in prison he interpreted dreams for two men. What were the occupations of these two men?

_____

Trivia Questions for the Expert

1. What Bible personality was called a half-baked pancake?

   _____

2. What was the name of the king who put Jeremiah into a dungeon in which he sank in the mire?

   _____

3. Absalom caught his hair in what kind of a tree?

   _____

4. Four rivers flowed out of the Garden of Eden. What are the names of these four rivers?

   _____

5. Eldad and Medad are famous because of:
   a. Their victory in battle   b. Their prophecy
   c. Their rebellion against Moses
   d. Not in the Bible

6. Muppim, Huppim, and Ard were:
   a. Amramite gods   b. The words of a chant of the priest of Baal   c. Three men who rebelled
   d. The sons of Benjamin   e. Not in the Bible

7. What was the name of the man who had his head cut off and thrown over a wall to Joab?

   _____

8. What tribe had 700 left-handed men who could sling stones at a hairbreadth and not miss?

9. What was the name of the secretary of Paul the apostle who wrote the book of Romans for Paul?

10. At Belshazzar's feast a hand wrote on the wall, "Mene, Mene, Tekel, Upharsin." What was the interpretation of the words?

11. What were the weather forecasts Jesus told the Pharisees and Sadducees?

12. Who was the person called Candace?

13. When the seventh seal was opened in the book of Revelation, there was silence in heaven for:
    a. A minute   b. A half-hour   c. An hour
    d. A day   e. A month   f. A half-year
    g. A year

14. In His ministry, Jesus mentioned a region of ten cities. What was that region called?

15. What was the name of Blind Bartimaeus's father?

16. In what book of the Bible does God tell a certain man not to cover his mustache?

17. When Aaron's rod blossomed, what type of nuts did it yield?

18. On the priestly garments a certain fruit was used as a design. What kind of fruit was it?

_____

19. The Old Testament character Job lived in the land of _____.

20. Who had faces like lions and could run as fast as the gazelles?

_____

21. What does the word Ebenezer mean?

_____

22. Who fell asleep during a sermon and died as a result?

_____

23. When the Ark of the Covenant was being brought back to Jerusalem, the oxen shook the cart and the Ark started to turn over. One man put his hand on the Ark to keep it from falling and died as a result of touching the Ark. Who was this man?

_____

24. What is the shortest verse in the Old Testament?

_____

25. Who were the people called the Zamzummims?

_____

26. The first archer mentioned in the Bible was _____.

27. There are four different colored horses mentioned in the book of Revelation. What were the four different colors?

_____

28. What Bible character called himself "a dead dog"?

_____

29. What evangelist had four daughters who prophesied?

30. What is the longest word in the Bible?

31. What king slept in a bed that was four cubits (six feet) wide and nine cubits (thirteen feet) long?

32. In the book of Revelation a star called _____ fell when the third angel sounded his trumpet.

33. What boy king had to be hidden in a bedroom for six years to escape the wrath of his wicked grandmother?

34. The giant Goliath lived in what city?

35. How many proverbs is King Solomon credited in knowing?

36. Who washed his steps with butter?

37. Jeremiah had a secretary. What was his name?

38. Who in the Bible is considered the father of all musicians?

39. What is the name of the dressmaker who was raised from the dead?

40. What Bible character's hair stood up on end when he saw a ghost?

41. Naomi had two daughters-in-law. One daughter-in-law, Ruth, went with Naomi and the other daughter-in-law, named _____, stayed in the country of Moab.

42. When Joshua destroyed Jericho he destroyed everyone in the city except for how many households?

43. In what book of the Bible do you find a verse that contains every letter except the letter "J"?

44. Most young men smile when they kiss a girl, but what Bible character wept when he kissed his sweetheart?

45. What man in the Bible killed sixty-nine (three score and nine) of his brothers?

46. How much money did the brothers of Joseph make when they sold Joseph into slavery?

47. What Bible-song composer is given credit for writing 1005 songs?

48. Who were Jannes and Jambres? a. Two of the spies to the Promised Land   b. Two priests in Israel
c. Two men who started a rebellion against Joshua
d. Two of Pharaoh's magicians
e. Two of the children of Reuben

49. In order to bind a contract, what Bible person took off his shoe and gave it to his neighbor?

50. What is the name of the five-year-old boy who was dropped by his nurse and became crippled for life?

51. What woman in the Bible gave a man butter and then killed him by driving a nail through his head?

52. Two lawyers are mentioned in the Bible. What are their names?

53. What is the name of the king who became herbivorous and ate grass like the oxen?

54. In what book of the Bible is bad breath mentioned?

55. How long did Noah remain in the Ark?

56. Who could use bows and arrows or sling stones with either the right or left hand?

57. Who killed a lion in a pit on a snowy day?

58. Who killed 300 men with his own spear?

59. Which Bible characters ate a book and thought it was sweet like honey?

60. Who was quoted for saying, "Is there any taste in the white of an egg?"

61. During what event in the Bible did dove manure sell for food?

62. How many different arks are mentioned in the Bible?

63. What Bible character was mentioned as being the first craftsman with brass and iron?

64. What is the shortest chapter in the Bible?

65. What is the name of the individual who ate a little book and got indigestion?

66. Adam called his helpmate woman and he named her Eve. What did God call Eve?

67. What Bible character walked around naked and without shoes for three years?

68. What is the name of the man who was killed by having a nail driven through his head?

69. Who said, "Eli, Eli, Lama sabachthani," and what does it mean?

70. The Bible characters Samson, David, and Benaiah all have one thing in common. What is it?

71. What was the name of the man who killed 800 men with a spear?

72. Jesus had how many brothers and sisters?

73. Who was the man to kill 600 men with an ox goad?

74. What man in the Bible wished that he had been aborted?

75. The ministering women gave up their brass mirrors to make a bathtub for men to wash in. Who were these men?

76. What man in the Bible had hair like eagle feathers and nails like bird claws?

77. How many people in the Bible have their name beginning with the letter "Z"?

78. What was the name of the king who practiced divination by looking in a liver?

79. How many men in the Bible are named Dodo?

80. What was used to join the tabernacle curtains together?

81. What was the name of the eight-year-old boy who served as king of Jerusalem for 100 days?

82. What man tore his clothes and pulled out his hair because of interracial marriage?

83. What man tore out other men's hair for interracial marriage?

84. Who was the first bigamist mentioned in the Bible?

_____

85. What was the name of the judge in Israel who was a polygamist?

_____

86. What event caused a donkey's head to be sold for eighty pieces of silver?

_____

87. In what book of the Bible does it talk about camels wearing necklaces?

_____

88. Who fashioned five mice out of gold?

_____

89. In what portion of the Bible does it talk about the sole of a dove's foot?

_____

90. Who was the first drunkard to be talked about in the Bible?

_____

91. In what book of the Bible does it talk about men who neighed after their neighbors' wives?

_____

92. In the Old Testament 42,000 men were killed for the incorrect pronunciation of one word. What was that word?

_____

93. What Bible character shot an arrow through a man's body and who was the man who died?

_____

94. What is the name of the man who fed seventy kings at his table?

_____

95. Who got so hungry that she ate her own son?

96. What was Queen Esther's other name?

97. There is one place in the Bible where it talks about grease. In what book of the Bible do you find that comment?

98. In what book of the Bible does it command brides to shave their heads and manicure their nails?

99. According to Matthew, who were Joses, Simon, Judas and James?

100. Who killed a seven-and-a-half-foot tall Egyptian giant?

101. Where is the swimmer's breaststroke mentioned in the Bible?

102. Twenty-seven thousand men were killed when a wall of a city fell on them. What was the name of the city where the wall was located?

103. What was the name of the man who killed a giant having twelve fingers and twelve toes?

104. What Bible character burned his son alive as a sacrifice?

105. What person in the Bible set fire to 300 foxes' tails?

106. What Bible character had neither a father or mother, is mentioned eleven times in Scripture, was not born and did not die?

107. The book of Proverbs lists four creatures that are small but exceedingly wise. What are these four creatures?

108. Who warned his enemies by cutting up a yoke of oxen and saying to them that if they did not submit to him, the same thing would happen to them?

109. After Jesus had risen from the dead, Peter was fishing and caught a large amount of fish in his net and brought them to Jesus. How many fish did Peter catch in his net?

110. What Bible prophet prophesied that men would eat their own flesh?

111. What person in the Bible said, "A living dog is better than a dead lion"?

112. Which king set fire to his own palace and died in the flames?

113. How many locks of hair did Delilah cut from Samson's hair?

114. The prophet Ahijah the Shilonite found _____ outside of Jerusalem and tore his new garment into _____ pieces.

115. What was the name of one of the two friends that met Jesus on the road to Emmaus after the resurrection?

116. The word "ball" is mentioned only one time in the Bible. In what book of the Bible do you find this word?

117. Jerusalem was also known by two other names. What are those names?

118. How many pieces of silver did the Philistines promise Delilah if she could find out the secret of Samson's strength?

119. Who saw the portraits of handsome young men and fell in love with what she saw?

120. Where do you find the longest verse in the Bible?

121. How did Michal, David's wife, help David to escape the king's messengers?

122. What prophet talked about a girl being exchanged for a drink (wine)?

123. What was the name of the Bible character who had seventy-eight wives and concubines who gave birth to eighty-eight children?

124. There was a certain king who had his women perfumed for a year before they came to him. What was his name?

125. Nahor's two eldest sons were named:
    a. Huz and Buz   b. Huz and Muz
    c. Buz and Muz   d. Fuz and Suz
    e. Huz and Fuz   f. Buz and Suz

Puns, Riddles, and
Humorous Trivia Questions

1. What was the name of Isaiah's horse?

    _____

2. Who was the first man in the Bible to know the meaning of rib roast?

    _____

3. Where does it talk about Honda cars in the Bible?

    _____

4. Who is the smallest man in the Bible?

    _____

5. Where in the Bible does it say that we should not play marbles?

    _____

6. How were Adam and Eve prevented from gambling?

    _____

7. Where does it say in the Bible that we should not fly in airplanes?

    _____

8. What did Noah say while he was loading all the animals on the Ark?

9. When did Moses sleep with five people in one bed?

10. Where in the Bible does it talk about smoking?

11. What was the first theatrical event in the Bible?

12. Where in the Bible does it say that fathers should let their sons use the automobile?

13. Why are there so few men with whiskers in heaven?

14. Who was the best financier in the Bible?

15. What simple affliction brought about the death of Samson?

16. What did Adam and Eve do when they were expelled from the Garden of Eden?

17. What are two of the smallest insects mentioned in the Garden of Eden?

18. In what place did the cock crow when all the world could hear him?

19. What were the Phoenicians famous for?

_____

20. Where was deviled ham mentioned in the Bible?

_____

21. Who introduced the first walking stick?

_____

22. Where is medicine first mentioned in the Bible?

_____

23. Where in the Bible does it suggest that men should wash dishes?

_____

24. Where did Noah strike the first nail in the Ark?

_____

25. Why was Moses the most wicked man in the Bible?

_____

26. What man in the Bible spoke when he was a very small baby?

_____

27. At what time of day was Adam born?

_____

28. What man in the Bible had no parents?

_____

29. Where is tennis mentioned in the Bible?

_____

30. Was there any money on Noah's Ark?

_____

31. Paul the apostle was a great preacher and teacher and earned his living as a tentmaker. What other occupation did Paul have?

_____

32. Why was Adam's first day the longest?

_____

33. Why was the woman in the Bible turned into a pillar of salt?

_____

34. What is the story in the Bible that talks about a very lazy man?

_____

35. Why didn't the last dove return to the Ark?

_____

36. Who was the most successful physician in the Bible?

_____

37. How do we know they used arithmetic in early Bible times?

_____

38. How long a period of time did Cain hate his brother?

_____

39. Who was the first electrician in the Bible?

_____

40. Who sounded the first bell in the Bible?

_____

41. How did Jonah feel when the great fish swallowed him?

_____

42. Why are a pair of roller skates like the forbidden fruit in the Garden of Eden?

_____

43. What does the story of Jonah and the great fish teach us?

44. Do you know how you can tell that David was older than Goliath?

45. What is the difference between Noah's Ark and an archbishop?

46. When did Ruth treat Boaz badly?

47. Where was Solomon's temple located?

48. Who was the fastest runner in the world?

49. If Moses were alive today, why would he be considered a remarkable man?

50. How do we know that Noah had a pig in the Ark?

51. Why did Moses cross the Red Sea?

52. Who was the most popular actor in the Bible?

53. Who was the most ambitious man in the Bible?

54. Who were the twin boys in the Bible?

55. Where is baseball mentioned in the Bible?

56. Who was the first person in the Bible to eat herself out of house and home?

57. Why was Job always cold in bed?

58. How were the Egyptians paid for goods taken by the Israelites when they fled from Egypt?

59. Why didn't they play cards on Noah's Ark?

60. In the story of the Good Samaritan, why did the Levite pass by on the other side?

61. Who was the straightest man in the Bible?

62. Which came first — the chicken or the egg?

63. When is high finance first mentioned in the Bible?

64. What is the only wage that does not have any deductions?

65 At what season of the year did Eve eat the fruit?

66. If Methuselah was the oldest man in the Bible (969 years of age), why did he die before his father?

67. What has God never seen, Abraham Lincoln seldom saw, and we see every day?

The Book of Parables

Recently I interviewed a _____ (teacher, student, or whoever) from _____ (name of church, school, or organization you are speaking to) and asked (him/her) some Bible questions. I could tell that he (or she) had really learned a great deal, so I asked him what his favorite book of the Bible was. He said, "The New Testament." I replied, "What part of the New Testament?" He said, "Oh, by far, I love the Book of Parables best." I said, "Would you kindly relate one of those parables to me?"

He said, "Once upon a time, a man went from Jerusalem to Jericho and fell among thieves. And the thieves threw him into the weeds. And the weeds grew up and choked that man. He then went on and met the Queen of Sheba and she gave that man a thousand talents of gold and silver and a hundred changes of raiment. He then got in his chariot and drove furiously to the Red Sea. When he got there, the waters parted and he drove to the other side.

"On the other side he drove under a big olive tree and got his hair caught on a limb and was left hanging there. He hung there many days and many nights and the ravens brought him food to eat and water to drink. One night while he was hanging there asleep his wife

Delilah came along and cut off his hair. And he dropped and fell on stony ground. And the children of a nearby city came out and said, 'Go up thou bald head, go up thou bald head.' And the man cursed the children and two she-bears came out of the woods and tore up the children.

"Then it began to rain and it rained for forty days and forty nights. And he went and hid himself in a cave. Later he went out and met a man and said, 'Come and take supper with me.' But the man replied, 'I cannot come for I have married a wife.' So he went out into the highways and byways and compelled them to come in, but they would not heed his call.

"He then went on to Jericho and blew his trumpet seven times and the city walls came tumbling down. As he walked by one of the damaged buildings in the city he saw Queen Jezebel sitting high up in a window and when she saw him she laughed and made fun of him. The man grew furious and said, 'Toss her down.' And they did. Then he said, 'Toss her down again.' And they did. They threw her down seventy times seven. And the fragments they gathered up were twelve baskets full. The question now is ... 'Whose wife will she be on the day of resurrection?'"

Answers to Easy Trivia Questions

1. How many men did Nebuchadnezzar see walking in the fiery furnace?
   A: Four—Daniel 3:25

2. What did Noah see in the sky?
   A: A rainbow—Genesis 9:11-17

3. "For whatsoever a man soweth, _____."
   A: That shall he also reap—Galatians 6:7

4. "But _____ found grace in the eyes of the Lord."
   A: Noah—Genesis 6:8

5. "Delilah said to _____ , Tell me, I pray thee, wherein thy great strength lieth."
   A: Samson—Judges 16:6

6. "Pride goeth before destruction, and a haughty spirit before _____."
   A: A fall—Proverbs 16:18

7. "Follow me and I will make you _____."
   A: Fishers of men—Matthew 4:19

8. "Come unto me, all ye that labor and are _____."
   A: Heavy laden, and I will give you rest—Matthew 11:28

9. What were the names of the three disciples who were on the Mount of Transfiguration with Jesus?
A: Peter, James, and John—Matthew 17:1

10. What was the name of the village that was known as the "City of David"?
A: Bethlehem—Luke 2:4

11. Who was Andrew's brother?
A: Peter—Matthew 10:2

12. "A soft answer turneth away _____."
A: Wrath—Proverbs 15:1

13. The disciples were told to be wise as _____ and harmless as _____.
A: Serpents, doves — Matthew 10:16

14. In what city did Joseph, Mary, and Jesus live?
A: Nazareth—Matthew 2:23

15. What country did Joseph, Mary, and Jesus flee to?
A: Egypt—Matthew 2:13

16. Where did the Wise Men come from?
A: The east—Matthew 2:1

17. In the parable of the ten virgins, how many were wise and how many were foolish?
A: Five wise and five foolish—Matthew 25:1,2

18. Where did Jesus perform His first miracle?
A: Cana of Galilee—John 2:11

19. John the Baptist had an interesting diet of what?
A: Locusts and wild honey—Matthew 3:1-4

20. In what book of the Bible do you find these words? "I am the living bread which came down from heaven; if any man eat of this bread, he shall live for ever."
A: John—John 6:51

21. Peter said to Jesus, "Thou shalt never wash _____."
    a. My hands   b. My feet   c. My hair
    d. My clothes   e. My cup
    A. "b," My feet—John 13:8

22. Who prayed three times a day at an open window?
    A: Daniel—Daniel 6:10

23. Who had an occupation as a tentmaker?
    A: Paul the apostle—Acts 18:1-3

24. Jesus was arrested in _____.
    A: The Garden of Gethsemane—Matthew 26:36

25. Who in the Bible could be called "The Lion Tamer"?
    A: Daniel—Daniel 6

26. John the Baptist was how much older than Jesus?
    A: About six months—Luke 1:24-27,36,56,57

27. Who in the Bible could carry the title "The Strong Man?"
    A: Samson—Judges 14–16

28. "If God be for us, _____?"
    A: Who can be against us — Romans 8:31

29. In what book of the Bible do you find the words, "There is no new thing under the sun"?
    A: Ecclesiastes—Ecclesiastes 1:9

30. According to the book of Proverbs, the beginning of knowledge is _____.
    A: Fear of the Lord—Proverbs 1:7

31. Who was the man who said, "Every kind of beasts, and of birds hath been tamed by mankind"?
    A: James—James 3:7

32. In what book of the Bible do you find the story of the burning bush?
    A: Exodus—Exodus 3:2-4

33. To whom did Jesus say, "Get thee behind me, Satan"?
    A: Peter —Matthew 16:23

34. Who prayed inside of a fish?
    A: Jonah—Jonah 2:1

35. What is the longest psalm in the Bible?
    A: Psalm 119

36. The wise man built his house on _____ and
    the foolish man built his house on _____.
    A: Rock, sand—Matthew 7:24-27

37. What was the name of the special food that God
    provided for the children of Israel during the forty
    years in the wilderness?
    A: Manna—Exodus 16:14,15

38. "I am _____ and _____, the begin-
    ning and the ending."
    A: Alpha and Omega—Revelation 1:8

39. In what book of the Bible do you find the fol-
    lowing words? "And there are also many other
    things which Jesus did, the which, if they should
    be written every one, I suppose that even the
    world itself could not contain the books that
    should be written."
    A: John—John 21:25

40. Who in the Bible could carry the title "The Wise
    King"?
    A: King Solomon—1 Kings 3-11

41. Bartimaeus was: a. Lame   b. Deaf   c. Blind
    d. Leprous
    A: "c," blind—Mark 10:46

42. Who owned a coat that had many colors?
    A: Joseph—Genesis 37:3

43. "I am the true _____ , and my Father is the
    husbandman."
    A: Vine—John 15:1

44. What Bible character was turned into a pillar of salt?
    A: Lot's wife—Genesis 19:15-26

45. What Bible character ate food that was given to the pigs?
    A: The prodigal son—Luke 15:11-16

46. What type of animal did Aaron fashion out of gold?
    A: A calf—Exodus 32:2-4

47. In what book of the Bible do you find the following words? "In my Father's house are many mansions."
    A: John—John 14:2

48. Who wrote with His finger on the ground?
    A: Jesus—John 8:6

49. Name the three gifts that the Wise Men from the East brought to Baby Jesus.
    A: Gold, frankincense, and myrrh—Matthew 2:11

50. "For what shall it profit a man, if he shall gain _____?"
    A: The whole world, and lose his own soul—Mark 8:36

51. How many books are in the New Testament?
    a. 23   b. 25   c. 27   d. 29
    A: "c," 27.

52. "Pray without _____."
    A: Ceasing—1 Thessalonians 5:17

53. Where in the Bible do you find the following words? "Behold, I stand at the door, and knock."
    A: Revelation—Revelation 3:20

54. Who said, "Silver or gold have I none, but such as I have give I thee"?
    A: Peter—Acts 3:6

55. What is the first lie to be recorded in the Bible?
A: The serpent to Eve: "Ye shall not surely die"—Genesis 3:4

56. "I can do all things through _____."
A: Christ which strengtheneth me—Philippians 4:13

57. How many books are in the Old Testament?
a. 33   b. 35   c. 37   d. 39
A: "d," 39.

58. The book of Hebrews tells us to entertain strangers because they might be _____.
A: Angels—Hebrews 13:2

59. "Let the word of Christ dwell in you _____."
A: Richly in all wisdom—Colossians 3:16

60. "Whatsoever ye do in word or deed, do all____."
A: In the name of Lord Jesus—Colossians 3:17

61. "The _____ of a good man are ordered by the Lord."
A: Steps—Psalm 37:23

62. "I am the good _____."
A: Shepherd—John 10:11

63. "Be not overcome of evil, but _____."
A: Overcome evil with good—Romans 12:21

64. "I am the _____ of the _____."
A: Light, world—John 8:12

65. "I am the _____, the _____, and the _____."
A: Way, truth, life—John 14:6

66. "I am the _____; by me if any man enter in, he shall be saved."
A: Door—John 10:9

67. "If thy right eye offend thee, _____."
A: Pluck it out, and cast it from thee—Matthew 5:29

68. Who in the Bible was called, "A man after mine own heart"?
A: David—Acts 13:22

69. Who said, "Every son that is born ye shall cast into the river, and every daughter ye shall save alive"?
A: Pharaoh—Exodus 1:22

70. To whom was the following said? "Loose thy shoe from off thy foot; for the place whereon thou standest is holy."
A: To Joshua—Joshua 5:15; To Moses—Exodus 3:5

71. "_____, and it shall be given you; _____, and ye shall find; _____, and it will be opened unto you."
A: Ask, seek, knock—Matthew 7:7

72. Who said, "When I was a child, I spake as a child, I understood as a child, I thought as a child"?
A: Paul—1 Corinthians 13:11

73. Who said, "How can a man be born when he is old"?
A: Nicodemus—John 3:4

74. "For the wages of sin is death; _____."
A: But the gift of God is eternal life through Jesus Christ our Lord—Romans 6:23

75. Who said, "By their fruits ye shall know them"?
A: Jesus—Matthew 7:20

76. Who said, "Almost thou persuadest me to be a Christian"?
A: Agrippa—Acts 26:28

77. In what book in the Bible do you find the following? "So Joseph died, being a hundred and ten years old."
A: Genesis—Genesis 50:26

78. Who said, "Who touched my clothes?"
A: Jesus—Mark 5:30

79. Of whom was the following spoken? "He was a murderer from the beginning, and abode not in the truth, because there is no truth in him."
A: Satan or the devil—John 8:44

80. What was the name of Abraham's wife?
A: Sarah—Genesis 17:15

81. In what book of the Bible do you find the laws concerning the eating of clean things?
A: Leviticus

82. In what book of the Bible do you find the phrase, "God is love"?
A: 1 John—1 John 4:8

83. "Thy word is a lamp unto my feet, and _____."
A: A light unto my path—Psalm 119:105

84. "For many are called, _____."
A: But few are chosen—Matthew 22:14

85. What is the shortest verse in the New Testament?
A: Jesus wept—John 11:35

86. "O death, where is thy sting?_____?"
A: O grave, where is thy victory—1 Corinthians 15:55

87. How did Judas indicate to the crowd who Jesus was?
A: By kissing him—Matthew 26:47-49

88. Who in the Bible could be called "Mr. Patience"?
A: Job—Job 1:42

89. To whom were the following words spoken? "Because thou has done this, thou are cursed."
A: To the serpent—Genesis 3:14

90. David's occupation before he became a king was _____.
A: A shepherd—1 Samuel 16:11-13

91. "And ye shall know the truth, and the truth shall
    _____."
    A: Make you free—John 8:32

92. What is greater than faith and hope?
    A: Charity (KJV) or love (NIV)—1 Corinthians
    13:13

93. What happens when the blind lead the blind?
    A: Both shall fall into the ditch—Matthew 15:14

94. To whom was the following comment made? "For
    God so loved the world, that he gave his only
    begotten Son, that whosoever believeth in him
    should not perish, but have everlasting life."
    A: Nicodemus—John 3:9-16

95. "For where two or three are gathered together in
    my name _____."
    A: There am I in the midst of them—Matthew
    18:20

96. In what book of the Bible do you find the fol-
    lowing words? "Let every thing that hath breath
    praise the Lord."
    A: Psalms—Psalm 150:6

97. Cain did what for a living?
    A: He was a tiller of the ground—Genesis 4:2

98. Peter did what for a living?
    A: He was a fisherman—Matthew 4:18

99. Which apostle was called Doubting _____?
    A: Thomas—John 20:24-29

100. Abel did what for a living?
    A: He was a keeper of sheep—Genesis 4:2

101. Joseph, the husband of Mary, did what for a living?
    A: He was a carpenter—Matthew 13:55

102. In what book of the Bible do you find the words, "Blessed is the man that walketh not in the counsel of the ungodly"?
A: Psalms—Psalm 1

103. "Speak; for thy servant _____."
A: Heareth—1 Samuel 3:10

104. In what book of the Bible do you find the words, "In the beginning was the Word and the Word was with God, and the Word was God"?
A: John—John 1:1

105. "The Lord is my strength and _____."
A: My shield—Psalm 28:7; my song—Exodus 15:2

106. Who said that even all the hairs on our head are numbered by God?
A: Jesus—Matthew 10:30

107. Paul told Timothy to take something for his stomach's sake. What was it?
A: A little wine—1 Timothy 5:23

108. "Greater love hath no man than this, _____."
A: That a man lay down his life for his friends—John 15:13

109. When did Jesus make more than a hundred gallons of very good wine?
A: At the Cana wedding—John 2:1-11

110. Who made clothes out of leaves that were sewed together?
A: Adam and Eve—Genesis 3:7

111. Who was the wife of Boaz?
A: Ruth—Ruth 4:13

112. Who in the Bible could be called "The Giant Killer"?
A: David—1 Samuel 17

113. Who was the oldest brother—Cain or Abel?
A: Cain—Genesis 4:1,2

114. Who gave Jesus some food to help feed the 5000?
A: A lad—John 6:9

115. Who said, "My soul doth magnify the Lord ... he hath regarded the low estate of his handmaiden ... all generations shall call me blessed"?
A: Mary—Luke 1: 46-48

116. Who said that, "I have fought a good fight, I have finished my course, I have kept the faith"?
A: Paul—2 Timothy 4:7

117. What was the name of the man who gave each man in his army of 300 a trumpet and an empty pitcher?
A: Gideon—Judges 7:15,16

118. Who took golden earrings and made them into a calf?
A: Aaron—Exodus 32:2-4

119. Jesus said, "Peace, be still." Whom was He addressing?
A: He spoke to the stormy waters—Mark 4:37-39

120. "Saul hath slain his thousands, and David his ___."
A: Ten thousands—1 Samuel 18:7,8

121. What was Paul's other name?
A: Saul—Acts 13:9

122. Jesus mixed something with clay and put it on the eyes of the blind man to make him see. What did Jesus mix with the clay?
A: Spittle—John 9:6

123. When the Roman soldiers pierced Jesus in the side with a spear, what came out?
A: Water and blood—John 19:34

124. "For what is a man profited, if he shall gain the whole world, and lose his own _____?"
A: Soul—Matthew 16:26

125. Did Judas Iscariot keep the betrayal money or did he give it back?
A: He gave it back—Matthew 27:3-5

126. The Spirit of God descended on Jesus in the form of a_____.
A: Dove—Matthew 3:16

127. "For the law was given by Moses, but grace and _____ came by Jesus Christ."
A: Truth—John 1:17

128. What did Ananias sell in order to get money to give to the apostles?
A: Land—Acts 5:1-3

129. Who said, "No prophet is accepted in his own country"?
A: Jesus—Luke 4:24

130. Water that Jesus turned into wine was in how many pots?
A: Six—John 2:6

131. Who was Jesus talking about when He said, "I have not found so great a faith, no, not in Israel"?
A: The centurion—Luke 7:2-10

132. "Go ye therefore, and teach all nations, baptizing them_____."
A. In the name of the Father, and of the Son, and of the Holy Ghost—Matthew 28:19

133. "Judge not, _____."
A: That ye be not judged—Matthew 7:1

134. Who brought back to life the son of the widow in whose house he was staying?
A: Elijah—1 Kings 17:17-22

Answers to Fairly Easy Trivia Questions

1. What was the name of the prophet who was very hairy and wore a leather belt?
   A: Elijah—2 Kings 1:8

2. What is the name of the man who King David arranged to have killed because he wanted his wife?
   A: Uriah—2 Samuel 11:2-17

3. The earth, seas, grass, herb yielding seed, and the tree yielding fruit were created on which day of creation?   a. 2nd   b. 3rd   c. 4th   d. 5th
   A: "b," 3rd—Genesis 1:10-13

4. What was the name of the man who inherited Elijah's mantle?
   A: Elisha—2 Kings 2:12,13

5. What was the name of the man who owned a seamless coat?
   A: Jesus—John 19:23

6. What was the name of a man who worked seven years to earn a wife?
   A: Jacob—Genesis 29:20

7. What Bible prophet said, "Behold, a virgin shall conceive, and bear a son, and shall call his name Immanuel"?
   A: Isaiah—Isaiah 7:14

8. How old was Joseph when he was given his coat of many colors?
A: 17—Genesis 37:2,3

9. What was the name of the high priest's servant who had his ear cut off by the apostle Peter?
A: Malchus—John 18:10

10. What was the name of the Bible character who was blind and killed 3000 people while at a religious feast?
A: Samson—Judges 16:23,27-30

11. What was the name of the Jewish man who called himself greater than King Solomon?
A: Jesus—Matthew 12:42

12. After David knocked Goliath to the ground with a stone from his sling, he cut off Goliath's head with his own sword. True or false?
A: False. David cut off Goliath's head with Goliath's own sword—1 Samuel 17:50,51

13. What nation of people got sick and tired of eating quail for dinner?
A. The nation of Israel—Numbers 11:32,33

14. Which came first—the plague of lice or the plague of frogs?
A: The plague of frogs—Exodus 8:1-18

15. What was the name of the Bible prophet who was fed by birds?
A: Elijah—1 Kings 17:1-6

16. About whom was the following statement made? "Among those that are born of women there is not a greater prophet than____"?
A: John the Baptist—Luke 7:28

17. On what mountain did Noah's Ark come to rest?
A: Ararat—Genesis 8:4

18. What was the name of the queen who came from a far country to witness for herself the wisdom of King Solomon?
    A: The Queen of Sheba—1 Kings 10:1-10

19. What was the name of the man who wore clothes made out of camel's hair?
    A: John the Baptist—Matthew 3:1,4

20. At whose command were 300 pitchers broken?
    A: Gideon—Judges 7:16,19

21. How many days was Saul blind while in Damascus?
    A: Three—Acts 9:8,9

22. Who were the people who found frogs on their beds and in their ovens?
    A: The Egyptians—Exodus 8:3,6

23. Who said, "Divide the living child in two, and give half to the one, and half to the other"?
    A: Solomon—1 Kings 3:15,25

24. What was the name of the Bible character who was a cupbearer to a king and also an engineer?
    A: Nehemiah—Nehemiah 1:11; 2:5

25. What was the name of the man who came to Jesus by night to talk with him?
    A: Nicodemus—John 3:1,2

26. How old was Methuselah when he died?
    A: 969 years old—Genesis 5:27

27. Name the fruit of the Spirit.
    A: Love, joy, peace, longsuffering, gentleness, goodness, faith, meekness, temperance (self-control)—Galatians 5:22,23

28. How many windows were in Noah's Ark?
    A: One—Genesis 6:16

29. What was the name of the man who was released from prison by an angel?
    A: Peter—Acts 12:5-11

30. In what book of the Bible do you find the words, "Of making many books there is no end"?
A: Ecclesiastes—Ecclesiastes 12:12

31. What were the names of the two disciples who were called, "The Sons of Thunder"?
A: James and John—Mark 3:17

32. In order to see Jesus more clearly, Zacchaeus climbed what type of tree?
A: A sycamore tree—Luke 19:2-4

33. What was the name of the man who escaped from Damascus in a basket?
A: Saul (Paul)—Acts 9:23-25

34. How many people were saved in Noah's Ark?
A: Eight—Genesis 6:10,18

35. What was the name of the man who issued the decree that all the world should be taxed?
A: Caesar Augustus—Luke 2:1

36. What was the name of the tree that Adam and Eve were told not to eat fruit from?
A: The tree of the knowledge of good and evil—Genesis 2:17

37. What was the name of the man who foretold of the seven good years and the seven lean years in Egypt?
A: Joseph—Genesis 41:15,25,29,30

38. What was the name of the first woman judge in Israel?
A: Deborah—Judges 4:4

39. What was the name of the couple who died because they lied to the Holy Spirit?
A: Ananias and Sapphira —Acts 5:1-10

40. Who was accused of eating in the cornfields on the Sabbath?
A: Jesus—Luke 6:1,2

41. The Israelites were bitten by _____ and were healed by looking at the same creature made out of brass.
    A: Serpents—Numbers 21:9

42. Moses had a brother. What was his name?
    A: Aaron—Exodus 7:1

43. How many times did Samuel go to Eli the priest, thinking that Eli had called him?
    A: Three times—1 Samuel 3:4-8

44. What was the name of the queen who was devoured by dogs?
    A: Jezebel—1 Kings 16:30-31; 2 Kings 9:36

45. How old was Joseph when his brothers sold him into slavery?
    A: 17—Genesis 37:2,28

46. What is the name of the angel who told Mary that she would be the mother of Jesus?
    A: Gabriel—Luke 1:26

47. How many years did the children of Israel eat manna?
    A: Forty years—Exodus 16:35

48. How many years did God give Noah to build the Ark?
    A: 120 years—Genesis 6:3

49. How many stories or levels were in the Ark?
    A: Three—Genesis 6:16

50. What was the name of the father who was struck dumb, because of unbelief, until his son was born?
    A: Zacharias—Luke 1:13,18,20

51. What was the name of the man who had to work many years and got two wives as a result?
    A: Jacob—Genesis 29:16-28

52. What was in the Ark in the Tabernacle?
    A: The Ten Commandments, Aaron's rod, and a pot of manna—Hebrews 9:4

53. The Bible talks of a very tiny seed that becomes a very large tree. What is the name of the seed?
    A: Mustard—Matthew 13:31,32

54. How many Marys are mentioned in the Bible?
    A: Six—Mary the mother of Jesus—Matthew 2:11 and many passages; Mary Magdalene—Matthew 27:56 and many passages; Mary the mother of James and Joses—Matthew 27:56; Mary the sister of Martha—John 11:12; Mary the wife of Cleophas —John 19:25; and the Mary Paul greeted in Romans 16:6

55. What was the name of the woman who was called "The Seller of Purple"?
    A: Lydia—Acts 16:14

56. What is the last line of the Twenty-third Psalm?
    A: And I will dwell in the house of the Lord for ever—Psalm 23:6

57. Jesus said that He would rebuild the temple in how many days?
    A: Three—John 2:19

58. The manger is to Jesus as the basket in the bulrushes is to _____.
    A: Moses—Exodus 2:3,10

59. Who said, "Repent ye: for the kingdom of heaven is at hand"?
    A: John the Baptist—Matthew 3:1-2

60. On what mountain did Moses receive the law?
    A: Sinai—Exodus 24:12-16

61. Who replaced Moses as the leader of the children of Israel?
    A: Joshua—Joshua 1:1-9

62. To whom was the following statement made?
    "Take nothing for your journey, neither staves,

nor scrip, neither bread, neither money; neither have two coats apiece."
A: The twelve disciples—Luke 9:1-3

63. Timothy's mother was a Jewess and his father was_____.
A: Greek—Acts 16:1

64. What color was Esau's complexion? a. Pale
b. Light brown   c. Red   d. Black   e. White
A: "c," red—Genesis 25:25

65. What color was the robe that Jesus wore when the soldiers taunted Him?
A: Purple—John 19:2

66. Genesis is to Malachi as Matthew is to _____.
A: Revelation (first book to last in Old Testament; first book to last in New Testament)

67. Matthew, Mark, and John called it Golgotha or the place of the skull. What did Luke call it?
A: Calvary—Luke 23:33

68. In what book of the Bible do you find the words, "Make haste, my beloved, and be thou like to a roe or to a young hart upon the mountains of spices"?
A: Song of Solomon— Song of Solomon 8:14

69. In what book of the Bible do you find the words, "Be strong and of good courage"? a. Job
b. Philippians   c. Joshua   d. Ephesians
A: "c," Joshua—Joshua 1:6,9

70. Who said, "I am innocent of the blood of this just person"?
A: Pilate—Matthew 27:24

71. How many hours was Jesus on the cross?
A: Six —Mark 15:25,34-37

72. What was the relationship of Zebedee to James and John?
A: Father—Matthew 4:21

73. In what book of the Bible do you find the words, "Blessed are the meek: for they shall inherit the earth"?
A: Matthew—Matthew 5:5

74. In what book of the Bible do you find the Ten Commandments?
A: Exodus—Exodus 20:3-17

75. Who said, "He was oppressed, and he was afflicted, yet he opened not his mouth"?   a. Isaiah
b. Jeremiah   c. Ezekiel   d. Hosea
A: "a," Isaiah—Isaiah 53:7

76. Who was born first—Jacob or Esau?
A: Esau—Genesis 25:25,26

77. The spies who spied out the land of Canaan said that it flowed with _____ and _____.
A: Milk and honey—Numbers 13:27

78. Who was stoned to death for preaching that Jesus was the Savior?
A: Stephen—Acts 7:55-60

79. "It is easier for a _____ to go through the eye of a _____, than for a _____ to enter into the kingdom of God."
A: Camel, needle, rich man—Matthew 19:24

80. In the parable of the ten virgins, five of them were wise and five were foolish. Why were the foolish ones foolish?
A: They brought no oil for their lamps—Matthew 25:1-3

81. Who were the disciples who argued about sitting on the right- and left-hand sides of Jesus?
A: James and John—Matthew 10:2, 20:20-24

82. Who witnessed the conversation between Moses, Elijah, and Jesus?
A: Peter, James, and John—Matthew 17:1-3

83. On what day of creation were the sun, the moon, and the stars created?
A: The fourth day—Genesis 1:14-19

84. Paul and Barnabas had an argument over a certain man traveling with them on their missionary journey. What was that man's name?
A: John Mark—Acts 15:37-39

85. What were the names of the two spies who spied out Canaan Land and gave a favorable report?
A: Joshua and Caleb—Numbers 14:6-9

86. What Bible character was renamed Israel?
A: Jacob—Genesis 32:28

87. What preacher was mad because his preaching caused a whole city to repent?
A: Jonah—Jonah 3:1-5; 4:1

88. On what day of creation were the sea creatures and fowl created?
A: The fifth day—Genesis 1:20-23

89. Who saw Satan fall from heaven?
A: Jesus—Luke 10:17,18

90. What had a wrestling match with God and won?
A: Jacob—Genesis 32:24-30

91. Which came first, "Thou shalt not kill" or "Thou shalt not steal"?
A: Thou shalt not kill—Exodus 20:13,15

92. What was the name of the apostle who was shipwrecked three different times?
A: Paul—2 Corinthians 11:25

93. On which day of creation were the land animals and man created?
A: The sixth day—Genesis 1:24-31

94. What Bible character had 300 concubines?
A: King Solomon—1 Kings 11:1,3

95. What was the name of a physician in the Bible who was also an author?
A: Luke—Colossians 4:14

96. Who sold their younger brother into slavery?
A: The brothers of Joseph—Genesis 37:26-28

97. Lot escaped from the city of Sodom with whom?
A: His two daughters—Genesis 19:30

98. What was the name of the man who ordered the execution of 450 priests?
A: Elijah—1 Kings 18:22,40

99. Which book in the Bible was written to an "Elect Lady"?
A: 2 John—2 John 1:1

100. Jesus said that it was proper to pay tribute (money) to what man?
A: Caesar—Mark 12:14-17

101. Simon Peter cut off the ear of the high priest's servant. Which ear did he cut off?
A: Right ear—John 18:10

102. What Bible character said, "A little leaven leaveneth the whole lump"?
A: Paul—1 Corinthians 5:6; Galatians 5:9

103. How many years did Jacob work for his Uncle Laban in payment for his daughters?
A: Fourteen—Genesis 29:18-28

104. Who was healed—the son or the daughter of Jairus?
A: The daughter—Mark 5:22,23,35-42

105. "Blessed are the pure in heart: _____."
A: For they shall see God—Matthew 5:8

106. What book in the Bible has a warning against anyone adding to it or taking away from it?
A: Revelation—Revelation 22:18,19

107. What was the name of the man who lifted up the infant Jesus at the temple and praised God?
A: Simeon—Luke 2:25-31

108. In what book of the Bible do you find the following: "For the Lord himself shall descend from heaven with a shout, with the voice of the archangel"?
A: 1 Thessalonians 4:16,17

109. What sign was given to the shepherds at the time of Christ's birth?
A: A babe wrapped in swaddling clothes, lying in a manger—Luke 2:8,12

110. How many loaves and how many fishes did Jesus use to feed the 5000?
A: Five loaves and two fishes—Matthew 14:17-21

111. For what reason did the rich young ruler come to Christ?
A: For eternal life—Matthew 19:16

112. What does the name Emmanuel mean?
A: God with us—Matthew 1:23

113. What was the name of the king who sought to take the life of the baby Jesus?
A: Herod—Matthew 2:13

114. What was the name of the criminal who was released in place of Jesus?
A: Barabbas —Luke 23:18

115. What was the name of the mother of Abraham's first son?
A: Hagar—Genesis 16:15

116. What Bible character had a dream that his parents and brothers would bow down before him?
A: Joseph—Genesis 37:5-7

117. The city walls of _____ fell down when the trumpets were blown.
A: Jericho—Joshua 6:2-5

118. Name the two bodies of water that the children of Israel crossed on dry ground.
A: The Red Sea and the Jordan River—Exodus 13:18; Joshua 1:2

119. Where in the Bible do you find the longest recorded prayer of Jesus?
A: John—John 17

120. What was Matthew's other name?
A: Levi—Mark 2:14, Luke 5:27

121. What is the first beatitude?
A: Blessed are the poor in spirit: for theirs is the kingdom of heaven—Matthew 5:3

122. Is Bethlehem located in Galilee or in Judea?
A: Judea—Matthew 2:1

123. Jesus said that there were two masters you could not serve at the same time. What were they?
A: God and mammon—Matthew 6:24

124. What was Sarah's other name?
A: Sarai—Genesis 17:15

125. Who said, "Am I my brother's keeper?"
A: Cain—Genesis 4:9

126. Who said, "The Lord gave, and the Lord hath taken away; blessed be the name of the Lord"?
A: Job—Job 1:21

127. Who owned a coat that was dipped in blood?
A: Joseph—Genesis 37:31

128. Who was bitten by a snake and shook it off into a fire and felt no harm?
A: Paul—Acts 28:3-5

129. Peter was told by Jesus to forgive his brother how many times?
A: Seventy times seven (490) times—Matthew 18:21,22

Answers to Fairly Difficult Trivia Questions

1. Name the man who kept some of the spoils after the battle of Jericho and brought punishment to Israel.
   A: Achan—Joshua 7:1

2. How many of Jesus' brothers wrote books of the Bible?
   A: Two, James and Jude—Matthew 13:55

3. What was the name of Hosea's wife?
   A: Gomer—Hosea 1:3

4. What woman in the Bible tried to seduce a handsome slave?
   A: Potiphar's wife—Genesis 39:1,7

5. What was the name of the king who made a speech and as a result was eaten by worms?
   A: Herod (Agrippa the First)—Acts 12:21-23

6. Miriam and Aaron were upset with Moses because he married a woman who was an _____.
   A: Ethiopian—Numbers 12:1

7. How many of the clean animals did Noah take into the Ark?
   A: Seven pairs of clean and one pair of unclean—Genesis 7:2

8. What was the name of a Bible character who told a riddle about a lion?
   A: Samson—Judges 14:12-14

9. There was a very rich man who was a disciple of Jesus. What was his name?
   A: Joseph of Arimathea—Matthew 27:57

10. What was the name of the queen who was thrown out of a window?
    A: Jezebel—2 Kings 9:30-33

11. Solomon said that something "biteth like a serpent, stingeth like an adder." What was it?
    A: Wine—Proverbs 23:31,32

12. What was the name of the city where King Ahasuerus lived?
    A: Shushan—Esther 1:2

13. David is to a sling as Samson is to _____.
    A: The jawbone of an ass—1 Samuel 17:40, Judges 15:16

14. How many times did Noah send the dove from the Ark?
    A: Three—Genesis 8:8-12

15. Who had shoes that lasted for forty years and did not wear out?
    A: The children of Israel in the wilderness—Deuteronomy 29:5

16. What is the name of the father who had two daughters married to the same man?
    A: Laban—Genesis 29:16-28

17. How many years were the Israelites in bondage as slaves?
    A: 400 years—Genesis 15:13

18. King Solomon had how many wives?
    A: 700 wives—1 Kings 11:1,3 (Maybe he wasn't so wise after all!)

19. Name the two men who entertained angels unaware.
    A: Abraham and Lot—Genesis 18:1-22; 19:1-22

20. What was the name of the prophet who was swept away by a whirlwind?
    A: Elijah—2 Kings 2:11

21. The Sabeans took his oxen and his donkeys, the lightning killed his sheep, the Chaldeans stole his camels, and his servants were killed. To whom did all these things happen?
    A: Job—Job 1:14-19

22. Who dreamed about a ladder which reached up to heaven?
    A: Jacob—Genesis 28:10-12

23. To whom were the following words addressed? "Get thee out of thy country, and from thy kindred, and from thy father's house, unto a land that I will shew thee."
    A: Abram—Genesis 12:1

24. What Bible character was called "The Gloomy Prophet"?
    A: Jeremiah—Jeremiah 25:11

25. The man called Gehazi was a: a. Prophet b. Servant c. King d. Lawyer e. Wicked priest
    A: b," servant—2 Kings 4:12

26. What is the name of the first of the twelve disciples to be murdered?
    A: James—Acts 12:1,2

27. David the shepherd was how old when he became King of Israel?
    A: Thirty years old—2 Samuel 5:4

28. Who owned dishes that were pure gold?
    A: King Solomon—1 Kings 10:21

29. Someone came to Pilate and begged for the body of the crucified Jesus. Who was he?
    A: Joseph of Arimathea—Matthew 27:57,58

30. In what book of the Bible do you find the following words? "For God shall bring every work into judgment, with every secret thing, whether it

be good, or whether it be evil."
A: Ecclesiastes—Ecclesiastes 12:14

31. What was Lot's relationship with Abraham?
A: His nephew—Genesis 12:5

32. What is the name of the town that is called "City of Palm Trees"?
A: Jericho—Deuteronomy 34:3

33. Shem is to Noah as David is to _____.
A: Jesse (son to father)—Genesis 5:32; Acts 13:22

34. What was Jacob's relationship to Laban?
A: Nephew and son-in-law—Genesis 28:1,2; 29:16-28

35. What is the name of the first New Testament martyr?
A: John the Baptist—Matthew 14:10

36. Name the pool that had five porches.
A: The pool at Bethesda—John 5:2

37. Which came first—the Tower of Babel or the Flood?
A: The Flood—Genesis 7–9; Genesis 11

38. Lazarus is to Jesus as Eutychus is to _____.
A: Paul (he raised from the dead to he who healed)—John 11:43-45; Acts 20:7-12

39. There was a silversmith in Ephesus by the name of

_____.
A: Demetrius—Acts 19:24

40. What is the name of the Bible character who preached in a valley full of dead men's bones?
A: Ezekiel—Ezekiel 37:1-14

41. How old was Joseph when Pharaoh made him a ruler?
A: Thirty years old—Genesis 41:46

42. Apollos was a: a. King   b. God
c. Learned Jew   d. Maker of tents
A: "c," learned Jew—Acts 18:24

43. What was the name of the man who helped an African to understand the Scriptures?
A: Philip—Acts 8:26-35

44. What Bible character used salt to purify drinking water?
A: Elisha—2 Kings 2:20-22

45. How old was Moses when he died?
A: 120 years old—Deuteronomy 34:7

46. Something very special happened to a certain man when he was 600 years old. Who was he and what happened?
A: Noah, and it began to rain—Genesis 7:11

47. How many times did the boy who Elisha raised from the dead sneeze?
A: Seven times—2 Kings 4:32-35

48. The Ark that Noah built was thirty cubits high, fifty cubits wide, and _____ cubits long.
A: 300 cubits long—Genesis 6:15

49. Who said, "This day is this scripture fulfilled in your ears"?
A: Jesus—Luke 4:14,21

50. What Bible character ate a poor widow's last meal?
A: Elijah—1 Kings 17:10-15

51. In what book of the Bible does it describe hail-stones weighing a talent each (about 80 pounds)?
A: Revelation—Revelation 16:21

52. How many years did it take to build the temple in Jesus' time?
A: Forty-six years—John 2:20

53. Who was the man who ordered a cup to be put into a sack of corn?
A: Joseph—Genesis 44:2

54. There are two orders of angels. Can you name them?
A: Cherubim—Genesis 3:24; Seraphim—Isaiah 6:2

55. Some angels came to speak with Lot. How many angels were there?
A: Two—Genesis 19:1

56. How many psalms are there in the Old Testament?
A: 150

57. What is the name of the Bible character whose handkerchiefs were used to heal people?
A: Paul—Acts 9:11,12

58. Joab was a: a. Scribe   b. Priest
c. King   d. Soldier   e. Servant
A: "d," soldier—2 Samuel 2:24-28

59. What is the name of the man who was called "The Supplanter"?
A: Jacob—Genesis 27:36

60. What relationship was Mordecai to Esther?
A: Cousin—Esther 2:5-7

61. What is the name of the boy who was sent out into the desert with his mother?
A: Ishmael—Genesis 16:15; 21:14

62. What is the name of the man who offered thirty changes of garments for solving a riddle?
A: Samson—Judges 14:12-18

63. What was the name of a leper who was also the captain of the host of the King of Syria?
A: Naaman—2 Kings 5:1

64. Who asked for the head of John the Baptist and got it?
A: The daughter of Herodias—Matthew 14:6-11

65. What are the three most famous heads of hair mentioned in the Bible?
A: Samson—Judges 16:17; Absalom—2 Samuel 14:25; the woman who wiped the tears from Jesus' feet with her hair—Luke 7:44

66. What was the name of the Egyptian who bought Joseph from the Midianites?
A: Potiphar—Genesis 37:28,36

67. One of Joseph's brothers said, "Let us not kill him." Who was that brother?
A: Reuben—Genesis 37:21-23

68. Who could be called the great hunter of the Bible?
(He also loved red meat.)
A: Esau—Genesis 25:25-28

69. The Gibeonites would have been killed by Joshua
if it had not been for their old clothes, old shoes,
and what kind of bread?
A: Dry and moldy bread—Joshua 9:3-5,12

70. When Joseph's brothers first came to Egypt, he put
them into jail for: a. 1 day   b. 2 days
c. 3 days   d. 4 days   e. 5 days   f. 6 days
A: "c," 3 days—Genesis 42:6,17

71. How many Herods are there in the Bible?
A: Three: Herod the Great—Matthew 2:1-20;
Herod Antipas—Matthew 14:1-11; Mark 6:16-28;
Luke 3:1-19; 9:7-9; 13:31; 23:7-15; Acts 4:27;
Herod Agrippa the First—Acts 12:1-23

72. What type of wood did Noah use when he built
the Ark?
A: Gopher wood—Genesis 6:14

73. How many elders did Moses appoint to help him
share the load of dealing with the children of
Israel?
A: Seventy—Numbers 11:16,17

74. Who wrote the book of Lamentations?
A: Jeremiah

75. What three young men had a father who was 500
years old?
A: Ham, Shem, and Japheth: the sons of Noah—
Genesis 5:32

76. There was a certain group of men who could not
wear garments that would cause them to sweat.
Who were these men?
A: The priests of Israel—Ezekiel 44:15-18

77. Abraham asked God to spare the city of Sodom if
a certain number of righteous people lived there.

What was the final figure that God said He would spare the city for?
A: Ten righteous people—Genesis 18:32

78. In whose tomb was Jesus buried?
A: Joseph of Arimathaea—Matthew 27:57-60

79. What was the name of the woman who cast her young son in the bushes to die?
A: Hagar—Genesis 21:14,15

80. What was the name of the mother who hid her son in the bulrushes?
A: Jochebed, the mother of Moses—Exodus 2:3; 6:20

81. Jesus cursed three cities. What were their names?
A: Chorazin, Bethsaida, and Capernaum—Matthew 11:21-23

82. What was the name of the country in which Jesus healed two demon-possessed individuals?
A: Gadarenes or Gergesenes—Matthew 8:28

83. How many loaves of bread did Jesus use in feeding the 4000?
A: Seven—Matthew 15:36-38

84. Abraham left what country?
A: Ur of the Chaldees—Genesis 11:31

85. When Philip met the Ethiopian eunuch, he was reading from what book in the Old Testament?
A: Isaiah—Acts 8:27-30

86. Paul preached on Mars' Hill. In what city is Mars' Hill located?
A: Athens—Acts 17:15,22

87. Into how many parts did the soldiers divide Jesus' garments?
A: Four parts—John 19:23

88. What was the name of Jacob's firstborn child?
A: Reuben—Genesis 35:23

89. When Jacob followed Esau out of his mother's womb, he was holding onto what?
A: Esau's heel—Genesis 25:23-26

90. What happened to Jacob when he wrestled with God?
A: He became lame—Genesis 32:24-31

91. How many times did the children of Israel march around the city of Jericho?   a. 2   b. 7   c. 13   d. 21   e. 49
A: "c," 13—Joshua 6:1-4

92. What was the name of the wilderness in which John the Baptist preached?
A: Judea—Matthew 3:1

93. What caused the large fish to vomit Jonah onto dry land?
A: God spoke to the fish—Jonah 2:10

94. Who cast down his rod before Pharaoh and the rod became a serpent?
A: Aaron—Exodus 7:10

95. Who said, "The dog is turned to his own vomit again"?
A: Peter—2 Peter 2:20-22

96. "At midnight _____ and _____ prayed, and sang praises unto God; and the prisoners heard them."
A: Paul, Silas—Acts 16:25

97. God opened the mouth of a donkey and the donkey spoke to _____.
A: Balaam—Numbers 22:28

98. What was the name of the centurion from Caesarea who was part of the Italian band?
A: Cornelius—Acts 10:1

99. What was the name of Aquila's wife?
A: Priscilla—Acts 18:2

100. What was the name of the man who carried the cross for Jesus?
A: Simon the Cyrene—Matthew 27:32

101. To whom was the following spoken? "Go near, and join thyself to this chariot."
A: Philip—Acts 8:29

102. What was the name of Timothy's mother?
A: Eunice—2 Timothy 1:5

103. Paul the Apostle was born in what city?
A: Tarsus—Acts 9:11

104. What was the name of the prophet who foretold that Jesus would be born in Bethlehem?
A: Micah—Micah 5:2

105. What relationship was Lois to Timothy?
A: His grandmother—2 Timothy 1:5

106. "As it is written, _____ have I loved, but _____ have I hated."
A: Jacob, Esau—Romans 9:13

107. What is the name of the Old Testament prophet who foretold the virgin birth?
A: Isaiah—Isaiah 7:14

108. To whom was the following spoken? "Silver and gold have I none; but such as I have give I thee: In the name of Jesus Christ of Nazareth rise up and walk."
A: Peter was speaking to the lame beggar at the temple—Acts 3:1-6

109. What is the name of the woman who hid two Israelite spies on the roof of her house?
A: Rahab—Joshua 2:1-6

110. What Bible character saw a city coming down out of heaven?
A: John—Revelation 21:2

Answers to Hard Trivia Questions

1. Who was hung on a gallows fifty cubits (about seventy-five feet) high?
   A: Haman—Esther 7:9,10

2. What were the names of the first and last judges of Israel?
   A: Othniel—Judges 1:13; 3:9; and Samuel—1 Samuel 7:8

3. Who was the individual who watched over baby Moses while he floated in the bulrushes?
   A: His sister—Exodus 2:4

4. What was the name of the mother who made a little coat for her son every year?
   A: Hannah—for Samuel—1 Samuel 1:20; 2:18,19

5. What Bible prophet spoke of the killing of the children?
   A: Jeremiah—Jeremiah 31:15

6. What type of bird did Noah first send forth from the Ark?
   A: A raven—Genesis 8:6,7

7. The name of David's first wife was _____.
   A: Michal—1 Samuel 18:27

8. The title written above Jesus' cross said, "JESUS OF NAZARETH THE KING OF THE JEWS." Name the three languages that the title was written in.
A: Greek, Latin, and Hebrew—John 19:19,20

9. Because of Achan's sin he was stoned in the valley
_____.
A: Achor—Joshua 7:24-26

10. What was the name of the sorcerer who was struck blind by Paul the apostle?
A: Elymas—Acts 13:6-12

11. After Paul's shipwreck he swam to the island of __.
A: Melita—Acts 27:41-44; 28:1

12. What was the name of the wife of both Nabal and King David?
A: Abigail—1 Samuel 25:3,42

13. Which of Joseph's brothers was left behind as a hostage when the other nine returned to bring Benjamin to Egypt?
A: Simeon—Genesis 42:18-20,24

14. In order to win the battle with Amalek, Aaron and Hur helped Moses by _____.
A: Holding up his hands—Exodus 17:11-13

15. Zipporah had a very famous husband. What was his name?
A: Moses—Exodus 2:21

16. What was the name of the wife of Lapidoth and what is she famous for?
A: Deborah, and she was the first woman judge of Israel—Judges 4:4,5

17. When David scrabbled on the doors of the gate, and let spittle fall down on his beard, and pretended to be crazy, he was doing so because he was afraid of _____.
A: Achish, the king of Gath—1 Samuel 21:12-15

18. In what book of the Bible do you find the following words: "As a jewel of gold in a swine's snout . . ."?
    A: Proverbs—Proverbs 11:22

19. What was Nebuchadnezzar's son's name?
    A: Belshazzar—Daniel 5:2

20. "The Lord had made all things for himself: yea, even the wicked for _____."
    A: The day of evil—Proverbs 16:4

21. Hannah was the mother of Samuel. What was the name of Hannah's husband?
    A: Elkanah—1 Samuel 1:8

22. Whom did God tell to go and marry a prostitute?
    A: Hosea—Hosea 1:2

23. What is the name of the Bible character who saw a roll flying in the sky?
    A: Zechariah—Zechariah 5:1

24. Two men in the Bible had the same name. One was a very poor man and the other was a friend of Jesus. What was their common name?
    A: Lazarus—Luke 16:20; John 11;12:1

25. When Peter was released from prison, he knocked at the door of the gate and a certain person came to answer his knock. Who was that individual?
    A: Rhoda—Acts 12:13

26. People will be thrown into the lake of fire because _____.
    A: Their names are not written in the Book of Life—Revelation 20:15

27. When Paul was shipwrecked on the island of Melita, he stayed with the chief man on the island. Who was this man?
    A: Publius—Acts 28:1,7

28. What is the name of the man who slept in the land of Nod?
A: Cain—Genesis 4:16

29. "And they gave forth their lots; and the lot fell upon _____; and he was numbered with the eleven apostles."
A: Matthias—Acts 1:26

30. What was the name of the vagabond Jewish exorcists who tried to cast the evil spirit out of a man? "And the man in whom the evil spirit was leaped on them, and overcame them, and prevailed against them, so that they fled out of that house naked and wounded."
A: The seven sons of Sceva—Acts 19:13-16

31. "And Cush begat _____. He was a mighty hunter before the Lord."
A: Nimrod—Genesis 10:8,9

32. What was the name of the queen that was replaced by Esther?
A: Vashti—Esther 1:17

33. What Bible character was called "The Tishbite"?
A: Elijah—1 Kings 17:1

34. Who in the Bible asked God to put his tears in a bottle?
A: David—Psalm 56:8

35. What was the name of the archangel who debated with the devil?
A: Michael—Jude 9

36. What does the word Ichabod mean?
A: The glory is departed—1 Samuel 4:21

37. The apostle Peter was known by three other names. What were they?
A: Cephas—John 1:42; Simon—Matthew 10:2; Simeon—Acts 15:14

38. What was the name of the runaway slave who went back to his master?
A: Onesimus—Philemon 10-12

39. Who said, "Am I a dog, that thou comest to me with staves"?
A: Goliath—1 Samuel 17:43

40. What is the name of the partially blind man who was ninety-eight years old and was very fat who fell off his seat and broke his neck?
A: Eli—1 Samuel 4:15,18

41. What is the shortest verse in the Bible?
A: Jesus wept—John 11:35

42. What Bible character accidentally hanged himself in a tree?
A: Absalom—2 Samuel 18:9,10

43. How many children did Jacob have?   a. 9   b. 11   c. 13   d. 15   e. 17
A: "c," 13—Genesis 29,30,35 (twelve sons, one daughter)

44. How many days was Noah on the Ark before it started to rain?
A: Seven—Genesis 7:1,4

45. What type of bird fed the prophet Elijah?
A: A raven—1 Kings 17:1,6

46. What is the longest chapter in the Bible?
A: Psalm 119 with 176 verses

47. In what book of the Bible do you find the following words: "Can the Ethiopian change his skin, or the leopard his spots"?
A: Jeremiah—Jeremiah 13:23

48. When a certain king put on a feast, God's handwriting appeared on the wall and startled everyone present. What is the name of this king?
A: Belshazzar—Daniel 5

49. What is the name of the woman who slept at the feet of her future husband?
A: Ruth—Ruth 3:7-9; 4:10

50. What type of food did the brothers of Joseph eat after they threw him into the pit?
A: Bread—Genesis 37:23-25

51. A scarlet cord in a window saved someone and their family. Who was this person?
A: Rahab—Joshua 2:1,18

52. In a contest for good-looking men, four men won because they were vegetarians and God blessed them. Who were these men?
A: Daniel, Hananiah, Mishael, and Azariah—Daniel 1:11-16

53. Elisha cursed forty-two children because they made fun of him and mocked him. What did they say?
A: "Go up, thou bald head; go up, thou bald head"—2 Kings 2:15,23

54. As a result of the curse of Elisha, what happened to the forty-two children?
A: Two she-bears came out of the woods and tore them apart—2 Kings 2:15,23,24

55. When God expelled Adam and Eve from the Garden of Eden, he placed Cherubim at the _____ of the Garden of Eden.
A: East—Genesis 3:24

56. What Bible character drove his chariot furiously?
A: Jehu—2 Kings 9:20

57. What is the name of the left-handed Benjamite who killed King Eglon?
A: Ehud—Judges 3:15-25

58. King Eglon was killed with a dagger that was _____ inches long, and the dagger could not

be pulled out because _____.
A: About eighteen inches long (one cubit), because Eglon was so fat that the fat closed upon the blade so that he could not draw the dagger out of his belly—Judges 3:22

59. What two books in the Bible were written to Theophilus?
A: Luke and Acts—Luke 1:3; Acts 1:1

60. What Bible character had his lips touched with a live coal?
A: Isaiah—Isaiah 6:6,7

61. Who was the person who dreamed about a tree which reached to heaven?
A: Nebuchadnezzar—Daniel 4:4,5,10,11

62. What woman in the Bible had five husbands?
A: The woman of Samaria (or the woman at the well)—John 4:7,17,18

63. When the magi came to seek the baby Jesus, where did they find him?
A: In a house—Matthew 2:1,2,11

64. Who caused bricklayers to go on strike?
A: Moses—Exodus 1:13,14; 4:29; 5:1; 12:51

65. What Bible character changed dust into lice?
A: Aaron—Exodus 8:17

66. Who was the man to first organize an orchestra in the Bible?
A: David—2 Samuel 6:5

67. Of all the books in the Bible, which one does not contain the name of God?
A: Esther

68. A lost ax head was made to float by _____.
A: Elisha—2 Kings 6:5-7

69. What person in the Bible walked for forty days without eating?
   A: Elijah—1 Kings 19:2,8

70. Why did Absalom kill his brother Amnon?
   A: Because he raped Tamar—2 Samuel 13:10-32

71. Who paid for the nursing of Moses?
   A: Pharaoh's daughter—Exodus 2:8,9

72. Who committed suicide with his own sword?
   A: Saul—1 Samuel 31:1-5

73. Who committed suicide by hanging himself?
   A: Judas Iscariot—Matthew 27:3-5

74. What king pouted in his bed because he could not buy someone's vineyard?
   A: Ahab—1 Kings 21:2-4

75. King Solomon had another name. What was it?
   A: Jedidiah—2 Samuel 12:24,25

76. Who was the man to build the first city and what was its name?
   A: Cain, and the name of the city was Enoch—Genesis 4:17

77. What woman in the Bible made a pair of kid gloves for her son?
   A: Rebekah—Genesis 27:15,16

78. A certain queen's blood was sprinkled on horses. Who was this queen?
   A: Jezebel—2 Kings 9:30-33

79. Who was the first musician in the Bible? What instruments did he play?
   A: Jubal, and he played the harp and organ—Genesis 4:21

80. What Bible person cut his hair only once a year?
   A: Absalom—2 Samuel 14:25,26

81. Name the gentile king that made Esther his queen.
    A: Ahasuerus—Esther 2:16,17

82. Who said the following and to whom was he speaking? "Because thou hast mocked me: I would there were a sword in mine hand, for now would I kill thee."
    A: Spoken by Balaam to his donkey—Numbers 22:28,29

83. The mother-in-law of Ruth was Naomi. What was the name of her father-in-law?
    A: Elimelech—Ruth 1:2-4

84. Which man committed adultery with his daughter-in-law after she diguised herself as a harlot? What was her name?
    A: Judah, Tamar—Genesis 38:13-18

85. How many times did Balaam hit his donkey before the donkey spoke to him?
    A: Three times—Numbers 22:28

86. How many years were added to Hezekiah's life?
    A: Fifteen—Isaiah 38:5

87. Joash was told to shoot an arrow from the window. What was the arrow called?
    A: The arrow of the Lord's deliverance—2 Kings 13:15-17

88. God gave Hezekiah a sign that he would live longer. What was that sign?
    A: The shadow on the sundial went backward ten degrees—Isaiah 38:8

89. Name the king who had the longest reign in the Bible.
    A: Manasseh (fifty-five years)—2 Chronicles 33:1

90. Which of the prophets was thrown into a dungeon?
    A: Jeremiah—Jeremiah 37:16

91. When a certain king tried to take the place of the priest at the altar, he was struck with leprosy. Who was this king?
A: Uzziah—2 Chronicles 26:18-21

92. How was Naaman healed of his leprosy?
A: He dipped seven times in the Jordan River—2 Kings 5:1,10,14

93. While _____ was hanging in a tree, he was killed by three darts from Joab.
A: Absalom—2 Samuel 18:14

94. Nicodemus put how many pounds of myrrh and aloes on the body of Jesus?
A: One hundred pounds—John 19:39

95. What was the name of the person who became king while he was a little child?
A: Josiah—2 Kings 22:1

96. Job's friends sat in silence with Job and mourned with him for how many days?
A: Seven days—Job 2:11,13

97. Where was Judas Iscariot buried?
A: In a potter's field—Matthew 27:3-10

98. Jesus told Nathanael that he had seen him before. Where did Jesus see Nathanael?
A: Under a fig tree—John 1:48

99. In the book of Proverbs, God says He hates how many things?
A: Seven things (a proud look, a lying tongue, hands that shed innocent blood, a wicked heart, someone willing to be mischievous, a false witness, and someone who sows discord)—Proverbs 6:16

100. The Bible suggests that the average life span is how many years?
A: Seventy—Psalm 90:10

101. How many barrels of water did Elijah ask the men to pour over the sacrifice on the altar?
A: Twelve—1 Kings 18:33,34

102. Because of offering "strange fire" on the altar of God, how many men died?
A: Two—Leviticus 10:1,2

103. David disobeyed God and numbered the people. As a result, how many punishment choices did God give David? a. 2   b. 3   c. 4   d. 5
A: "b," 3—1 Chronicles 21:10

104. What leader chose his followers by watching how they drank water?
A: Gideon—Judges 7:5

105. How many stones were placed in the Jordan River after the children of Israel had crossed over on dry land?
A: Twelve—Joshua 4:3

106. As Joshua and the children of Israel marched around the walls of Jericho, the priests carried trumpets before the Ark of the Lord. How many priests carried trumpets?
A: Seven—Joshua 6:4

107. When Elijah was on Mt. Carmel, how many times did he send his servant to look for a cloud?
A: Seven—1 Kings 18:42-44

108. The two spies that Rahab hid fled into the mountains and hid for how many days?
A: Three days—Joshua 2:3,22

109. How many men from the tribe of Judah were sent out to capture Samson?
A: Three thousand—Judges 15:11

110. How old was Jehoash when he was crowned king?
A: Seven years old—2 Kings 11:21

111. This person was brought water from the well at Bethlehem but poured it out on the ground because it was brought to him at great risk. Who was this person?
A: David—2 Samuel 23:15,16

112. What type of bird was sold for "two for a farthing"?
A: Sparrow—Matthew 10:29

113. Absalom was riding on a _____ when his hair caught in a tree.
A: Mule—2 Samuel 18:9

114. What did Achan steal from Jericho?
A: Gold, silver, and a garment—Joshua 7:1,21

115. What Old Testament character wore a "coat of mail"?
A: Goliath—1 Samuel 17:4,5

116. Name the twelve apostles.
A: Peter, Andrew, James, John, Philip, Bartholomew (Nathaniel), Thomas, Matthew, James, Thaddaeus, Simon, Judas Iscariot—Matthew 10:1-4

117. What was the name of the witch that Saul visited?
A: The witch of Endor—1 Samuel 28:7

118. The word "coffin" is used only once in the entire Bible. Do you know who was buried in this coffin?
A: Joseph—Genesis 50:26

119. The Bible warns men to beware of a woman's eyes. In what book of the Bible do you find this warning?
A: Proverbs—Proverbs 6:25

120. While Joseph was in prison he interpreted dreams for two men. What were the occupations of these two men?
A: Baker and butler—Genesis 40:1-9,16

Answers to Trivia Questions for the Expert

1. What Bible personality was called a half-baked pancake?
   A: Ephraim ("Ephraim is a cake not turned") —Hosea 7:8

2. What was the name of the king who put Jeremiah into a dungeon in which he sank in the mire?
   A: Zedekiah—Jeremiah 38:5,6

3. Absalom caught his hair in what kind of a tree?
   A: Oak—2 Samuel 18:9

4. Four rivers flowed out of the Garden of Eden. What are the names of these four rivers?
   A: Pison, Gihon, Hiddekel, and Euphrates—Genesis 2:10-14

5. Eldad and Medad are famous because of:
   a. Their victory in battle   b. Their prophecy
   c. Their rebellion against Moses
   d. Not in the Bible
   A: "b," their prophecy—Numbers 11:26-29

6. Muppim, Huppim, and Ard were:
   a. Amramite gods   b. The words of a chant of the priest of Baal   c. Three men who rebelled
   d. The sons of Benjamin   e. Not in the Bible
   A: "d," the sons of Benjamin—Genesis 46:21

7. What was the name of the man who had his head cut off and thrown over a wall to Joab?
   A: Sheba—2 Samuel 20.11 22

8. What tribe had 700 left-handed men who could sling stones at a hairbreadth and not miss?
   A: The Benjamites—Judges 20:15,16

9. What was the name of the secretary of Paul the apostle who wrote the book of Romans for Paul?
   A: Tertius—Romans 16:22

10. At Belshazzar's feast a hand wrote on the wall, "Mene, Mene, Tekel, Upharsin." What was the interpretation of the words?
    A: *Mene*—God hath numbered thy kingdom, and finished it; *Tekel*—Thou art weighed in the balances, and art found wanting; *Upharsin*—Thy kingdom is divided, and given to the Medes and Persians—Daniel 5:25-28

11. What were the weather forecasts Jesus told the Pharisees and Sadducees?
    A: Evening sky red—fair weather; morning sky red—stormy weather—Matthew 16:1-3

12. Who was the person called Candace?
    A: Queen of the Ethiopians—Acts 8:27

13. When the seventh seal was opened in the book of Revelation, there was silence in heaven for:
    a. A minute   b. A half-hour   c. An hour
    d. A day   e. A month   f. A half-year
    g. A year
    A: "b," a half-hour—Revelation 8:1

14. In His ministry, Jesus mentioned a region of ten cities. What was that region called?
    A: Decapolis—Matthew 4:25

15. What was the name of Blind Bartimaeus's father?
    A: Timaeus—Mark 10:46

16. In what book of the Bible does God tell a certain man not to cover his mustache?
    A: Ezekiel—Ezekiel 24:17

17. When Aaron's rod blossomed, what type of nuts did it yield?
A: Almonds—Numbers 17:8

18. On the priestly garments a certain fruit was used as a design. What kind of fruit was it?
A: Pomegranates—Exodus 28:2,34

19. The Old Testament character Job lived in the land of _____.
A: Uz—Job 1:1

20. Who had faces like lions and could run as fast as the roes (gazelles)?
A: The Gadites, part of David's mighty men—1 Chronicles 12:8

21. What does the word Ebenezer mean?
A: "Hitherto hath the LORD helped us"—1 Samuel 7:12

22. Who fell asleep during a sermon and died as a result?
A: Eutychus—Acts 20:9

23. When the Ark of the Covenant was being brought back to Jerusalem, the oxen shook the cart and the Ark started to turn over. One man put his hand on the Ark to keep it from falling and died as a result of touching the Ark. Who was this man?
A: Uzzah—2 Samuel 6:6,7

24. What is the shortest verse in the Old Testament?
A: Eber, Peleg, Reu—1 Chronicles 1:25

25. Who were the people called the Zamzummims?
A: A race of giants—Deuteronomy 2:20

26. The first archer mentioned in the Bible was ____.
A: Ishmael—Genesis 16:16; 21:14,20

27. There are four different colored horses mentioned in the book of Revelation. What were the four different colors?
A: White, red, black, pale—Revelation 6:1-8

28. What Bible character called himself "a dead dog"?
A: Mephibosheth—2 Samuel 9:6,8

29. What evangelist had four daughters who prophesied?
    A: Philip—Acts 21:8,9

30. What is the longest word in the Bible?
    A: Mahershalalhashbaz—Isaiah 8:1,3

31. What king slept in a bed that was four cubits (six feet) wide and nine cubits (thirteen feet) long?
    A: Og, the king of Bashan, who was a giant—Deuteronomy 3:11

32. In the book of Revelation a star called _____ fell when the third angel sounded his trumpet.
    A: Wormwood—Revelation 8:10,11

33. What boy king had to be hidden in a bedroom for six years to escape the wrath of his wicked grandmother?
    A: Joash—2 Kings 11:1,2

34. The giant Goliath lived in what city?
    A: Gath—1 Samuel 17:4

35. How many proverbs is King Solomon credited in knowing?
    A: Three thousand—1 Kings 4:30,32

36. Who washed his steps with butter?
    A: Job—Job 29:1,6

37. Jeremiah had a secretary. What was his name?
    A: Baruch—Jeremiah 36:10,17,18

38. Who in the Bible is considered the father of all musicians?
    A: Jubal—Genesis 4:21

39. What is the name of the dressmaker who was raised from the dead?
    A: Dorcas—Acts 9:36-40

40. What Bible character's hair stood up on end when he saw a ghost?
    A: Eliphaz—Job 4:1,15,16

41. Naomi had two daughters-in-law. One daughter-in-law, Ruth, went with Naomi and the other

daughter-in-law, named _____, stayed
in the country of Moab.
A: Orpah—Ruth 1:4,14

42. When Joshua destroyed Jericho he destroyed everyone in the city except for how many households?
A: One—Joshua 6:17

43. In what book of the Bible do you find a verse that
contains every letter except the letter "J"?
A: Ezra—Ezra 7:21

44. Most young men smile when they kiss a girl, but
what Bible character wept when he kissed his
sweetheart?
A: Jacob—Genesis 29:11,18

45. What man in the Bible killed sixty-nine (three
score and nine) of his brothers?
A: Abimelech, son of Gideon—Judges 9:4,5

46. How much money did the brothers of Joseph
make when they sold Joseph into slavery?
A: Twenty pieces of silver—Genesis 37:28

47. What Bible-song composer is given credit for
writing 1005 songs?
A: Solomon—1 Kings 4:30,32

48. Who were Jannes and Jambres?   a. Two of the
spies to the Promised Land   b. Two priests in
Israel   c. Two men who started a rebellion
against Joshua   d. Two of Pharaoh's magicians
e. Two of the children of Reuben
A: "d," two of Pharaoh's magicians—2 Timothy
3:8

49. In order to bind a contract, what Bible person took
off his shoe and gave it to his neighbor?
A: Boaz for Ruth—Ruth 4:7-10

50. What is the name of the five-year-old boy who was
dropped by his nurse and became crippled for life?
A: Mephibosheth—2 Samuel 4:4

51. What woman in the Bible gave a man butter and then killed him by driving a nail through his head?
   A: Jael—Judges 5:24-26

52. Two lawyers are mentioned in the Bible. What are their names?
   A: Gamaliel and Zenas—Acts 5:34; Titus 3:13

53. What is the name of the king who became herbivorous and ate grass like the oxen?
   A: King Nebuchadnezzar—Daniel 4:33

54. In what book of the Bible is bad breath mentioned?
   A: Job—Job 19:17

55. How long did Noah remain in the Ark?
   A: One year and seventeen days (seven days were before it started to rain)—Genesis 7:10,11; 8:13,14

56. Who could use bows and arrows or sling stones with either the right or left hand?
   A: David's mighty men—1 Chronicles 12:1,2

57. Who killed a lion in a pit on a snowy day?
   A: Benaiah, son of Jeholada—1 Chronicles 11:22

58. Who killed 300 men with his own spear?
   A: Abishai, brother of Joab—1 Chronicles 11:20

59. Which Bible characters ate a book and thought it was sweet like honey?
   A: Ezekiel—Ezekiel 2:9; 3:3; John—Revelation 10:9,10

60. Who was quoted for saying, "Is there any taste in the white of an egg?"
   A: Job—Job 6:6

61. During what event in the Bible did dove manure sell for food?
   A: During the famine in Samaria—2 Kings 6:25

62. How many different arks are mentioned in the Bible?
   A: Three: the Ark of Noah—Genesis 6:14; the ark

that Moses slept in—Exodus 2:3; the Ark of the Covenant—Numbers 10:33

63. What Bible character was mentioned as being the first craftsman with brass and iron?
A: Tubal-Cain—Genesis 4:22

64. What is the shortest chapter in the Bible?
A: Psalm 117 (two verses)

65. What is the name of the individual who ate a little book and got indigestion?
A: John the apostle—Revelation 10:10

66. Adam called his helpmate woman and he named her Eve. What did God call Eve?
A: Adam—Genesis 5:1,2

67. What Bible character walked around naked and without shoes for three years?
A: Isaiah—Isaiah 20:3

68. What is the name of the man who was killed by having a nail driven through his head?
A: Sisera, the Canaanite captain—Judges 4:18-21

69. Who said, "Eli, Eli, Lama sabachthani" and what does it mean?
A: Jesus, and it means, "My God, My God, why hast thou forsaken me?"—Matthew 27:46

70. The Bible characters Samson, David, and Benaiah all have one thing in common. What is it?
A: They all slew a lion—Judges 14:5,6; 1 Samuel 17:34-36; and 2 Samuel 23:20

71. What was the name of the man who killed 800 men with a spear?
A: Adino the Eznite—2 Samuel 23:8

72. Jesus had how many brothers and sisters?
A: Four brothers and at least two sisters—Mark 6:3

73. Who was the man to kill 600 men with an ox goad?
A: Shamgar —Judges 3:31

74. What man in the Bible wished that he had been aborted?
A: Job—Job 3:2,3,11,16

75. The ministering women gave up their brass mirrors to make a bathtub for men to wash in. Who were these men?
A: Moses, Aaron and his sons—Exodus 38:8; 40:30,31

76. What man in the Bible had hair like eagle feathers and nails like bird claws?
A: Nebuchadnezzar—Daniel 4:33

77. How many people in the Bible have their name beginning with the letter "Z"?
A: 188 different people, representing 87 different names, including 27 Zechaiahs, 12 Zichris, 9 Zebadiahs, 9 Zadoks, 7 Zabads, 7 Zaccurs, 7 Zerahs, and 5 Zedekiahs

78. What was the name of the king who practiced divination by looking in a liver?
A: The King of Babylon—Ezekiel 21:21

79. How many men in the Bible are named Dodo?
A: Three—Judges 10:1; 2 Samuel 23:9; 23:24

80. What was used to join the tabernacle curtains together?
A: Fifty gold taches (clasps)—Exodus 26:6

81. What was the name of the eight-year-old boy who served as king of Jerusalem for 100 days?
A: Jehoiachin—2 Chronicles 36:9

82. What man tore his clothes and pulled out his hair because of interracial marriage?
A: Ezra—Ezra 9:1-3

83. What man tore out other men's hair for interracial marriage?
A: Nehemiah—Nehemiah 13:23-25

84. Who was the first bigamist to be mentioned in the Bible?
A: Lamech—Genesis 4:19 (His penalty was two mothers-in-law!)

85. What was the name of the judge in Israel who was a polygamist?
A: Gideon—Judges 8:30

86. What event caused a donkey's head to be sold for eighty pieces of silver?
A: The famine in Samaria—2 Kings 6:25

87. In what book of the Bible does it talk about camels wearing necklaces?
A: Judges—Judges 8:21,26

88. Who fashioned five mice out of gold?
A: The Philistines—1 Samuel 6:1-5;16,18

89. In what portion of the Bible does it talk about the sole of a dove's foot?
A: In the story of Noah and the Ark—Genesis 8:9

90. Who was the first drunkard to be talked about in the Bible?
A: Noah—Genesis 9:20,21

91. In what book of the Bible does it talk about men who neighed after their neighbors' wives?
A: Jeremiah 5:8

92. In the Old Testament 42,000 men were killed for the incorrect pronunciation of one word. What was that word?
A: Shibboleth—Judges 12:5,6

93. What Bible character shot an arrow through a man's body and who was the man who died?
A: Jehu shot the arrow and Jehoram died—
2 Kings 9:24

94. What is the name of the man who fed seventy kings at his table?
A: Adonibezek—Judges 1:7

95. Who got so hungry that she ate her own son?
A: A woman of Samaria during the great famine —2 Kings 6:25,29

96. What was Queen Esther's other name?
A: Hadassah—Esther 2:7

97. There is one place in the Bible where it talks about grease. In what book of the Bible do you find that comment?
A: Psalms—Psalm 119:70

98. In what book of the Bible does it command brides to shave their heads and manicure their nails?
A: Deuteronomy—Deuteronomy 21:11,12

99. According to Matthew, who were Joses, Simon, Judas, and James?
A: The brothers of Jesus—Matthew 13:55

100. Who killed a seven-and-a-half-foot tall Egyptian giant?
A: Benaiah—1 Chronicles 11:22,23

101. Where is the swimmer's breaststroke mentioned in the Bible?
A: Isaiah ("As he that swimmeth spreadeth forth his hands to swim")—Isaiah 25:11

102. Twenty-seven thousand men were killed when a wall of a city fell on them. What was the name of the city where the wall was located?
A: Aphek—1 Kings 20:30

103. What was the name of the man who killed a giant having twelve fingers and twelve toes?
A: Jonathan, son of Shimeah—2 Samuel 21:20,21

104. What Bible character burned his son alive as a sacrifice?
A: Ahaz—2 Kings 16:2,3

105. What person in the Bible set fire to 300 foxes' tails?
A: Samson—Judges 15:4

106. What Bible character had neither a father or mother, is mentioned eleven times in Scripture, was not born and did not die?
A: Melchisedec—Hebrews 7:1-3

107. The book of Proverbs lists four creatures that are small but exceedingly wise. What are these four creatures?
A: Ants, conies (badgers), locusts, and spiders—Proverbs 30:24-28

108. Who warned his enemies by cutting up a yoke of oxen and saying to them that if they did not submit to him, the same thing would happen to them?
A: Saul—1 Samuel 11:7

109. After Jesus had risen from the dead, Peter was fishing and caught a large amount of fish in his net and brought them to Jesus. How many fish did Peter catch in his net?
A: One hundred fifty-three—John 21:11

110. What Bible prophet prophesied that men would eat their own flesh?
A: Isaiah—Isaiah 9:20

111. What person in the Bible said, "A living dog is better than a dead lion"?
A: Solomon—Ecclesiastes 1:1; 9:4

112. Which king set fire to his own palace and died in the flames?
A: Zimri—1 Kings 16:18

113. How many locks of hair did Delilah cut from Samson's hair?
A: Seven—Judges 16:18,19

114. The prophet Ahijah the Shilonite found _____ outside of Jerusalem and tore his new garment into _____ pieces.
A: Jeroboam, twelve pieces—1 Kings 11:29,30

115. What was the name of one of the two friends that met Jesus on the road to Emmaus after the resurrection?
A: Cleopas—Luke 24:13,18

116. The word "ball" is mentioned only one time in the Bible. In what book of the Bible do you find this word?
A: Isaiah—Isaiah 22:18

117. Jerusalem was also known by two other names. What are those names?
A: Jebus—Judges 19:10; Salem—Psalm 76:2

118. How many pieces of silver did the Philistines promise Delilah if she could find out the secret of Samson's strength?
A: Eleven hundred pieces of silver—Judges 16:5

119. Who saw the portraits of handsome young men and fell in love with what she saw?
A: Aholibah—Ezekiel 23:11-16

120. Where do you find the longest verse in the Bible?
A: Esther—Esther 8:7

121. How did Michal, David's wife, help David to escape the king's messengers?
A: She put a dummy in the bed—1 Samuel 19:12-16

122. What prophet talked about a girl being exchanged for a drink (wine)?
A: Joel—Joel 3:3

123. What was the name of the Bible character who had seventy-eight wives and concubines who gave birth to eighty-eight children?
A: Rehoboam—2 Chronicles 11:21

124. There was a certain king who had his women perfumed for a year before they came to him. What was his name?
A: Ahasuerus—Esther 2:12

125. Nahor's two eldest sons were named:
a. Huz and Buz b. Huz and Muz c. Buz and Muz
d. Fuz and Suz e. Huz and Fuz f. Buz and Suz
A: "a," Huz and Buz—Genesis 22:20,21

Answers to Puns, Riddles, and Humorous Trivia Questions

1. What was the name of Isaiah's horse?
   A: Is Me. Isaiah said, "Woe, is me."

2. Who was the first man in the Bible to know the meaning of rib roast?
   A: Adam

3. Where does it talk about Honda cars in the Bible?
   A: In Acts 1:14—"These all continued with one *accord.*"

4. Who is the smallest man in the Bible?
   A: Some people believe that it was Zacchaeus. Others believe it was Nehemiah (Ne-high-a-miah), or Bildad, the Shuhite (Shoe-height). But in reality it was Peter the disciple. He slept on his watch!

5. Where in the Bible does it say that we should not play marbles?
   A: In John 3:7—Jesus said to Nicodemus, "Marvel not..." (Marble-Not)

6. How were Adam and Eve prevented from gambling?
   A: Their paradise (pair-o-dice) was taken away from them.

7. Where does it say in the Bible that we should not fly in airplanes?
   A: In Matthew 28:20—"Lo (Low), I am with you always"...not high up in the air.

8. What did Noah say while he was loading all the animals on the Ark?
   A: "Now I herd everything."

9. When did Moses sleep with five people in one bed?
   A: When he slept with his forefathers.

10. Where in the Bible does it talk about smoking?
    A: In Genesis 24:64—Rebekah lighted off her camel.

11. What was the first theatrical event in the Bible?
    A: Eve's appearance for Adam's benefit.

12. Where in the Bible does it say that fathers should let their sons use the automobile?
    A: In Proverbs 13:24—"He that spareth his rod hateth his son."

13. Why are there so few men with whiskers in heaven?
    A: Because most men get in by a close shave.

14. Who was the best financier in the Bible?
    A: Noah. He floated his stock while the whole world was in liquidation.

15. What simple affliction brought about the death of Samson?
    A: Fallen arches.

16. What did Adam and Eve do when they were expelled from the Garden of Eden?
    A: They raised Cain.

17. What are two of the smallest insects mentioned in the Bible?
    A: The widow's "mite," and the "wicked flee" —Mark 12:42 and Proverbs 28:1.

18. In what place did the cock crow when all the world could hear him?
    A: On Noah's Ark.

19. What were the Phoenicians famous for?
    A: Blinds.

20. Where was deviled ham mentioned in the Bible?
    A: When the evil spirits entered the swine.

21. Who introduced the first walking stick?
    A: Eve . . . when she presented Adam a little Cain.

22. Where is medicine first mentioned in the Bible?
    A: Where the Lord gives Moses two tablets.

23. Where in the Bible does it suggest that men should wash dishes?
    A: In 2 Kings 21:13—"And I will wipe Jerusalem as a man wipeth a dish, wiping it, and turning it upside down."

24. Where did Noah strike the first nail in the Ark?
    A: On the head.

25. Why was Moses the most wicked man in the Bible?
    A: Because he broke the Ten Commandments all at once.

26. What man in the Bible spoke when he was a very small baby?
    A: Job. He cursed the day he was born.

27. At what time of day was Adam born?
    A: A little before Eve.

28. What man in the Bible had no parents?
    A: Joshua, the son of Nun.

29. Where is tennis mentioned in the Bible?
    A: When Joseph served in Pharaoh's court.

30. Was there any money on Noah's Ark?
    A: Yes. The duck took a bill, the frog took a greenback, and the skunk took a scent.

31. Paul the apostle was a great preacher and teacher and earned his living as a tentmaker. What other occupation did Paul have?
    A: He was a baker. We know this because he went to Philippi (Fill-a-pie).

32. Why was Adam's first day the longest?
    A: Because it had no Eve.

33. Why was the woman in the Bible turned into a pillar of salt?
    A: Because she was dissatisfied with her Lot.

34. What is the story in the Bible that talks about a very lazy man?
   A: The story about the fellow that loafs and fishes.

35. Why didn't the last dove return to the Ark?
   A: Because she had sufficient grounds to stay away.

36. Who was the most successful physician in the Bible?
   A: Job. He had the most patience (patients).

37. How do we know they used arithmetic in early Bible times?
   A: Because the Lord said to multiply on the face of the earth.

38. How long a period of time did Cain hate his brother?
   A: As long as he was Abel.

39. Who was the first electrician in the Bible?
   A: Noah, when he took his family and the animals out of the Ark it made the Ark light (arc light).

40. Who sounded the first bell in the Bible?
   A: Cain when he hit Abel.

41. How did Jonah feel when the great fish swallowed him?
   A: Down in the mouth.

42. Why are a pair of roller skates like the forbidden fruit in the Garden of Eden?
   A: They both come before the fall.

43. What does the story of Jonah and the great fish teach us?
   A: You can't keep a good man down.

44. Do you know how you can tell that David was older than Goliath?
   A: Because David rocked Goliath to sleep.

45. What is the difference between Noah's Ark and an archbishop?
   A: One was a high ark, but the other is a hierarch.

46. When did Ruth treat Boaz badly?
   A: When she pulled his ears and trod on his corn.

47. Where was Solomon's temple located?
   A: On the side of his head.

48. Who was the fastest runner in the world?
   A: Adam, because he was first in the human race.

49. If Moses were alive today, why would he be considered a remarkable man?
   A: Because he would be several thousand years old.

50. How do we know that Noah had a pig in the Ark?
   A: He had Ham.

51. Why did Moses cross the Red Sea?
   A: To avoid Egyptian traffic.

52. Who was the most popular actor in the Bible?
   A: Samson. He brought the house down.

53. Who was the most ambitious man in the Bible?
   A: Jonah, because even the great fish couldn't keep him down.

54. Who were the twin boys in the Bible?
   A: First and Second Samuel.

55. Where is baseball mentioned in the Bible?
   A: Genesis 1:1—In the beginning (big inning); Genesis 3:6—Eve stole first and Adam stole second; Genesis 24:15,16—Rebekah went to the well with a "pitcher"; Luke 15:11-32—The prodigal son made a home run; Judges—when Gideon rattled the pitchers; Exodus 4:4—"And he put forth his hand, and caught it"; Numbers 11:32—"ten homers"; Psalm 19:12—Who can understand my errors? Proverbs 18:10—"The righteous runneth into it, and is safe"; Ezekiel 36:12—"Yea, I will cause men to walk".

56. Who was the first person in the Bible to eat herself out of house and home?
   A: Eve.

57. Why was Job always cold in bed?
A: Because he had such miserable comforters.

58. How were the Egyptians paid for goods taken by the Israelites when they fled from Egypt?
A: The Egyptians got a check on the bank of the Red Sea.

59. Why didn't they play cards on Noah's Ark?
A: Because Noah sat on the deck.

60. In the story of the Good Samaritan, why did the Levite pass by on the other side?
A: Because the poor man had already been robbed.

61. Who was the straightest man in the Bible?
A: Joseph. Pharaoh made a ruler out of him.

62. Which came first—the chicken or the egg?
A: The chicken, of course. God doesn't lay any eggs.

63. When is high finance first mentioned in the Bible?
A: When Pharaoh's daughter took a little prophet (profit) from the bulrushes.

64. What is the only wage that does not have any deductions?
A: The wages of sin.

65. At what season of the year did Eve eat the fruit?
A: Early in the fall.

66. If Methuselah was the oldest man in the Bible (969 years of age), why did he die before his father?
A: His father was Enoch. Enoch never died, he was taken directly to heaven.

67. What has God never seen, Abraham Lincoln seldom saw, and we see every day?
A: Isaiah 40:25; 46:5—"'To whom then will ye liken me, or shall I be equal?' saith the Holy One." God has never seen His equal, Abraham Lincoln seldom saw his equal, and we see our equals every day.